Gill's Irish Lives

DANIEL O'CONNELL

GILL'S IRISH LIVES

DANIEL O'CONNELL

FERGUS O'FERRALL

GILL AND MACMILLAN

First published 1981 by
Gill and Macmillan Ltd
Goldenbridge
Dublin 8
with associated companies in
London, New York, Delhi, Hong Kong,
Johannesburg, Lagos, Melbourne,
Singapore, Tokyo

0 7171 1041 9 (paperback)
0 7171 1070 2 (hardback)

available in this series:
Michael Collins (Leon Ó Broin)
Sean O'Casey (Hugh Hunt)
C. S. Parnell (Paul Bew)
James Craig (Patrick Buckland)
James Joyce (Peter Costello)
Eamon de Valera (T. Ryle Dwyer)
Daniel O'Connell (Fergus O'Ferrall)
Theobald Wolfe Tone (Henry Boylan)
Edward Carson (A. T. Q. Stewart)
James Connolly (Ruth Dudley Edwards)
Arthur Griffith (Calton Younger)

Origination by Healyset, Dublin
Printed and bound in Great Britain by
Redwood Burn Ltd., Trowbridge, Wiltshire.

Contents

In Memory
George O'Ferrall
1902–1973

Acknowledgments

It is impossible to thank individually all the historians who have assisted my work on Daniel O'Connell; many of them have books included in the Bibliography which reveals how indebted this work is to their researches.

It is a pleasure to acknowledge the outstanding help which I received from Miss S. M. Parkes, of Trinity College, Dublin, in the course of my research. At Trinity, also, Professor J. V. Rice was a friend and mentor and to him I am most grateful.

This book is dedicated to the memory of my father who expressed in his life such a thorough enjoyment of people and of Irish rural life; to him I owe my interest in Irish history and literature. I can never repay my debt to my mother but I can acknowledge her decisive part in my education. I wish to thank my brothers Neil and Rory for their interest and help; Rory has lived with me and my work for so many years that I feel his contribution should be specially acknowledged. I owe a great deal to Fergal Tobin of Gill and Macmillan for his professional advice and valuable suggestions.

My greatest and increasing debt is to my wife, Iris, whose patience, understanding and hard work has made the production of this book possible; it is hers as much as mine.

February 1981

Fergus O'Ferrall,
Greystones, Co. Wicklow

Notes on References

Citations of letters from *The Correspondence of Daniel O'Connell*, ed. M. R. O'Connell, Vols I–VIII, are referenced in parentheses by volume number and number of letter. Thus, O'Connell to A. V. Kirwan, 11 December 1837, letter 2476 in Volume VI, is cited as (VI, 2476). Citations from other works listed in the Bibliography are referenced in parentheses by bibliography number (indicated in italic), volume number (where appropriate) and page number. Thus, a reference to page 273 from the first volume of W. Fagan, *The Life and Times of Daniel O'Connell,* 2 vols, Cork 1847–8 — which is listed as item number 29 in the Bibliography — will appear as (*29*, I, 273). All other sources are listed in the References and are indicated in the text by superior numbers. In all cases where reference is made to a book which has appeared in two or more editions, page numbers refer to the most recent edition.

Introduction

Daniel O'Connell, irritated with a writer who had attempted a biographical sketch of his career, pleaded for it to be 'remodelled according to truth, leaving out both the *fulsome flattery* and the *flagrant false-hood*' (VI, 2476). O'Connell sets his biographers a good standard but one especially difficult to achieve: during fifty years of political involvement, contro-versy raged around O'Connell; it pursued him to the tomb and has persisted ever since. His political career, especially to sympathetic writers, has seemed perplex-ing; some, such as Lecky, even questioned whether his life was a blessing or a curse on the Ireland he led. Yet, reflecting on O'Connell's enormous stature, no matter how his career may be interpreted, one is reminded of some great hero of antiquity: his colossal impact on the Irish people, his complex personality, courage with perseverance and the space he filled in the eyes of Europe and America bears out King Ludwig of Bavaria's contemporary assessment of O'Connell as 'that energetical character inseparable for ever from the history of our age'.

Thomas Hardy once wrote that 'War makes rattling good history; but Peace is poor reading.' In Ireland, the mere talk of war has made, if not 'good history', at least popular history; peace has not only been 'poor reading', some of it has never been written. The popular historiography which surrounds O'Connell depended, until recent decades, upon those who believed that war not only made 'good history' but [2] also created free nations.

O'Connell has received a 'bad press' despite the evidence that he has been one of the three decisive political figures in modern Ireland. No matter what the verdict on his career few have disputed the magnitude of his impact. His career involved issues still vital in modern Irish politics, particularly the role of violence in the struggle for Irish nationality; hence he remains a touchstone in Irish political development:

> The great mission of O'Connell's life has not merely been to gain Emancipation or to secure Repeal, but to drill, instruct, guide, habituate and organise the people so that the instinct of physical force may be rooted out; so that they may be thoroughly masters of the art of peaceful warfare: ... so that they may never dream of the insanity of shouldering arms to attain whatever results the nation thinks just and reasonable and vehemently desires for itself.

Frederick Lucas, who wrote this assessment in *The Tablet* in August 1846, pinpoints both the tragedy of O'Connell's life and his continued relevance. The tragedy stems from the failure of O'Connell's mission. The relevance is obvious: O'Connell realised that the means affect the end — how human liberation is attained determines whether it is true liberation or not.

Other questions arise. Was O'Connell in some way responsible for the Famine by his advocacy of 'moral force'? Did he foster Catholic sectarianism? Did he inaugurate a lowly type of demagogic politics which was priest-ridden, ultimately futile and devoid of social concern? Was he an enemy of the working class? Did he help to kill the Irish language by his utilitarianism? Was he sexually immoral — the kind of personality who could be immoral in politics as well?

Did he misjudge the importance of Young Ireland policies in the struggle for Irish freedom? [3]

This short biography is 'modelled according to truth' and the intention is to leave out 'both the fulsome flattery and the flagrant falsehood'. It does not pretend to be definitive but to rest upon the best available evidence and modern historical scholarship. It is written in the conviction that there is no single historical figure more important for Irish people to understand than Daniel O'Connell.

1
'The Grand Theatre of the World'

I have now two objects to pursue. The one, the attainment of knowledge; the other, the acquisition of all those qualities which constitute the polite gentleman. . . . I have indeed a glowing and (if I may use the expression) an enthusiastic ambition . . . If I do not rise at the bar I will not have to meet the reproaches of my own conscience. . . . Indeed as for my knowledge in the professional line that cannot be discovered for some years to come. But I have time in the interim to prepare myself to appear with greater *eclat* on the grand theatre of the world.

Daniel O'Connell to his uncle Maurice, 10 December 1795 (I, 18)

1

The young man in London who wrote, at the age of twenty, the unusual letter quoted above, had passed the first fifteen years of his life in West Kerry. These early years were decisive in shaping O'Connell's character and personality. As Sean O'Faolain has observed, Kerry was 'a hard place for hard men' and the O'Connell family 'were honestly realistic about their world'. The O'Connells were landowners of old Gaelic stock who had used the remoteness of Iveragh and Dunkerrin to survive and prosper, despite the penal code against their religion. Daniel's uncle

Maurice, nicknamed Hunting Cap, was the con-
solidator of the O'Connell smuggling and trading
'empire'; he played a decisive part in young Daniel's
life, adopting him and his brother Maurice as his
own heirs.

Daniel O'Connell, born on 6 August 1775, was the
eldest of ten children; his father Morgan ran a successful general store, farmed and engaged in business.
Morgan had married Catherine O'Mullane, a daughter
of John O'Mullane, a small Catholic landlord, near
Mallow, Co. Cork. O'Connell's parents lived at Carhen,
near Caherciveen, but he spent little time at this farm
house: the baby Daniel was nursed out to a peasant
family until he was four years old and when he
returned Hunting Cap adopted Morgan's two boys.
So Daniel was to spend the next ten years at the more
substantial Derrynane House, on the coast about
sixteen miles from Carhen.

Daniel O'Connell's youth was completely Gaelic;
he absorbed and thoroughly enjoyed the lifestyle of
Uíbh Ráthach (Iveragh), the mountainous and scenic
peninsula that lies between Dingle Bay and Kenmare
Bay. In the summer of 1795 Hunting Cap wrote an
amusing account of Daniel's activities to his mother:

Your son left this ten days ago and took with
him my favourite horse. Had it not been for that,
I might have dispensed with his company. He is, I
am told, employed in visiting the seats of hares at
Keelrelig, the earths of foxes at Tarmons, the caves
of otters at Bolus, and the celebration of Miss
Burke's wedding at Direen—useful avocations,
laudable pursuits, for a nominal student of the
law! The many indications he has given of a liberal
mind in the expenditure of money has left a
vacuum in my purse, as well as an impression on
my mind, not easily eradicated (*17*, II, 272).

O'Connell had a long life which was lived at very [6] different levels over a period of great change. He was influenced by the most diverse factors but in his youth and in his attachment to Kerry we find the first and most basic level on which he lived. He always returned to find relaxation and recreation in this Irish-speaking district which he loved: 'Next to you and my babes' he wrote his wife in March 1810, 'I love Iveragh'. For O'Connell it was always a return to his roots; as Professor John A. Murphy observes, it was 'a constant nourishing of his *dúchas* and a major element in his greatness'.[1]

O'Connell's forebears were among the limited number of Gaelic and Catholic landowning families which survived the turmoil and confiscations of previous centuries to emerge in the late eighteenth century still in possession of some considerable property. For the O'Connells, as for all in this Kerry 'Gaeltacht', survival was paramount. Hunting Cap was the great exemplar of the survival mentality. Pragmatism, intelligence, ruthlessness and industry were the required qualities. The O'Connell 'world' was cosmopolitan; it was said that they were familiar with seven languages — Irish, as their first tongue, English for correspondence, Latin and Greek as basic to their education, and French, German and Spanish as the second language of those O'Connells in the military service of the European powers. As a boy, Daniel had more than a dozen relatives holding commissions in the French army. One of his uncles, Daniel Charles, Count O'Connell, rose to the rank of general in the French army; another relative, Moritz, Baron O'Connell, was for nearly sixty years until his death in 1830 chamberlain to three Emperors of Austria. There were extensive trade links with the Continent in Hunting Cap's smuggling business and young Daniel and Maurice were to be sent for their education to France. The O'Connells transferred their monarchical leanings from the Stuarts to the House of Hanover in a pragmatic fashion and they constantly sought respectability, and that degree of social acceptance which matched their wealth. Hunting Cap was made a Justice of the Peace on the passing of the Catholic Relief Act in 1793 and he had no difficulty in supporting the Union because he looked, as did most Catholics, to the British government to secure Catholic rights; Catholics had experience enough of the Irish Protestant Ascendancy. The O'Connells, by virtue of their economic success, were both conservative and confident: conservative in that they had a great deal to lose in any political turmoil and confident in that they felt the equal of any Protestant. O'Connell's outrage at Protestant assumptions of superiority emerges in his famous attack on Saurin, the Attorney-General in 1813: 'I deny in the strongest terms his unfounded and absurd claim to superiority. I am his equal at least in birth — his equal in fortune — his equal certainly in education; and, as to talent, I should not add that, but there is little vanity in claiming equality'. The quest for equality was to be central in his life and politics.

Daniel O'Connell inherited this 'world' and shared, with his extensive family, a rich culture; he retained his 'Gaeltacht' personality which is revealed in his pragmatism, resourcefulness, and in his patriarchal, familial and lavish lifestyle. His politics soon diverged from those of his family and to discover why we must look to his education in France, London and Dublin.

2

A hedge-schoolmaster called David Mahony taught Daniel O'Connell his letters: 'I learned the alphabet in an hour', he told O'Neill Daunt long afterwards.

'I was in my childhood remarkably quick and per-
[8] severing. My childish propensity to idleness was overcome by the fear of disgrace. I desired to excel, and
could not brook the idea of being inferior to others.'
Then he was sent, with his younger brother Maurice,
in the summer of 1790, to Father Harrington's school
at Cove, near Cork; after six months Hunting Cap
arranged for the boys to attend the English College
at St Omer in France where he received a classical
education; after only a year there the President of
the College, Dr Stapylton, wrote to Hunting Cap a
report on Daniel's progress: 'I have but one sentence
to write about him, and that is that I never was so
much mistaken in my life as I shall be unless he is
destined to make a remarkable figure in society' (37,
16). Certainly Daniel's early letters to his wily old
uncle show a shrewdness and latent ability in the
teenager which confirms his headmaster's assessment.
St Omer was a preparatory school for the English
College at Douai and the O'Connells moved to Douai
in August 1792. They remained there only five
months, having to escape from revolutionary France
on the day the king was executed.

O'Connell left France probably confirmed in the
ancien régime politics of his family and with direct
experience of mob violence and the dangers of revolution. He continued his education in London under
Christopher Fagan, a friend of the O'Connell family,
and late in 1793 it was decided that he should pursue
a career in law. It had recently become possible for a
Catholic to become a barrister and in 1794 O'Connell
was enrolled in Lincoln's Inn on a slender enough
allowance from Hunting Cap. From this period he
began to prepare, in a very conscious fashion, for his
appearance 'on the great stage of the world' as he put
it in a letter to his uncle in January 1796. He became
aware of the great political events in a new way: in

1794 he attended the trial of Hardy, Secretary of the London Corresponding Society, for high treason, and this helped to convert him to popular opinions (*8, 50*). He read widely and began to keep a Journal which is now a fascinating record of the making of a radical. In a decade of extraordinary intellectual activity, O'Connell began reading, while they were still new, a number of epoch-making books and this contributed more than anything, save his West Kerry background, to the formation of his ideas. He became a member of the Honourable Society of Cogers where he says he acquired 'a great fluency of speech'; he became very conscious of how he spent his time and began to exercise that remarkable self-discipline which became such a feature of his career (*8*, 64). There is direct evidence in his Journal and letters that O'Connell sought to think out for himself a coherent political philosophy, 'a united train of ideas', and to overcome what he felt was 'an inherent shallowness of conception' (*8*, 76).

The self-education undertaken by O'Connell in this London period of his life between 1794 and 1796 was absolutely decisive in forming his basic political beliefs and outlook. He evidently read all the radical new political works but he was most impressed by William Godwin's *Inquiry Concerning Political Justice* written in 1793. O'Connell wrote in his Journal on 5 January 1796, about Godwin's book, 'I admire this work more, beyond comparison more, than any I ever met with. It has enlarged and strengthened my understanding, and infused into my mind a serenity never before enjoyed. In other words, it has made me a happier, and, I think, a better man' (*8*, 107). By the end of January he had finished Godwin and observed that his work could not 'be too highly praised'. From Godwin O'Connell took his political radicalism and also the belief that political reforms could best be

effected through moral force. Godwin had written in
[10] *Political Justice,* 'If the cause we plead be the cause
of truth, there is no doubt that by reasonings, if
sufficiently zealous and constant, the same purposes
may be effected in a mild and liberal way. In a word,
it is proper to recollect here what has been established
as to the doctrine of force in general, that it is in no
case to be employed but where every other means
is ineffectual.'

O'Connell was never a pacifist but he believed that
violence was inappropriate to the aim of true human
liberation: 'The altar of liberty totters when it is
cemented only with blood' he noted in his Journal
in December 1796. His ambition was to become a
leading figure in the struggle for the liberty of all
mankind; this aspiration was to stay with him
throughout his remarkable career though the crucible
of his Irish legal experience was to affect its expression. The phrase about the 'theatre of the world'
recurs in his Journal and letters at this period, probably reflecting his interest in the stage and his desire
to 'cut a great figure'. There was to be a great deal of
deliberate theatricalism in O'Connell's political campaigns. His romantic conception of how he would
pursue his political ambition mingled with his inherited
family pragmatism. Both romanticism and realism
provide vital clues to his subsequent political behaviour.

In January 1797 he writes in his Journal in the
romantic mode:

I would, and I trust I will serve man. I feel, I really
feel, the sacred and mild warmth of true patriotism.
I will endeavour to make the narrow circle of my
friends happy, I will endeavour to give cheerfulness
and ease to the peasantry over whom I may command, I will endeavour to give liberty to my country, and I will endeavour to increase the portion of
the knowledge and virtue of humankind.

O'Connell's reading in Godwin and Thomas Paine affected his religious outlook; in particular he came to feel that the best form of government is the one 'which laid fewest restraints on private judgment' (*8*, 102). He became a Deist for about ten or twelve years: in 1803 he writes to his wife, 'If I were a religionist I should spend every moment in praying for you — and this miserable philosophy which I have taken up and been proud of — in the room of religion, affords me now no consolation in my misery' (I, 85). Certainly by 1809, he had returned to the faith and practice of Catholicism; but he retained a permanent tolerance towards those who held different religious beliefs or no beliefs.

O'Connell returned to Dublin in December 1796 to keep terms at King's Inns so as to be called to the Irish Bar. He continued his wide reading in the Dublin Library, Eustace Street, and he attended and spoke in the Historical Society (*8*, 137, 156). He attended debates in the Irish parliament and conceived an ambition to become a member; in his politics he wished 'to avoid the profligacy of corruption and the violence of unreasonable patriotism' as he noted in his Journal in February 1797. O'Connell had imbibed the democratic principles of the American and French Revolutions but he had come to believe that real freedom for the people had to be acquired gradually, by moral means, rather than suddenly and by violence. Thus he was distressed at the prospect of revolution by the United Irishmen or invasion by the French: 'A revolution would not produce the happiness of the Irish nation' he observed in his Journal on 4 March 1797. He was also in danger as a young Catholic law student who held advanced political views. 'I must avoid disclosing my political sentiments so frequently as I do at present. It would be a devilish unpleasant thing to get *caged!*

Nonsense! *Liberality* can never become dangerous': [12] thus he debated with himself in his Journal on 31 March 1797. O'Connell probably destroyed portion of his Journal because of the opinions he had noted and he left Dublin in late June 1797 until the following November.

At this time, he suffered alternatively from real fear as to how events might turn out and great feelings of hope and elation at his own prospects. He joined the Lawyers' Artillery Corps in January 1797 as a volunteer, writing to his uncle that it was 'industriously propagated that such men as did not enter the corps would be marked by government' and it was obvious he was attracted by the glamour attached to the uniform, drilling and the general scent of excitement (I, 24a). O'Connell feared what a French invasion would mean: in January 1797 he wrote that if the December 1796 Bantry Bay invasion had been successful it would 'have shook the foundations of all property, would have destroyed our profession root and branch. All that I have read, all that I have thought, all that I have combined was about to be rendered nugatory at once. It was little. But this little was my all' (I, 25).

O'Connell had been associating with the United Irishmen in the debating society connected with the Dublin Library in Eustace Street and he sympathised with the objectives of civil rights and parliamentary reform. However, he clearly had no faith in violence and he was to condemn the United Irishmen for the loss of lives which they caused and for creating a context in which the Union could be carried. In his Journal he records on 2 January 1799 his feelings on 'the late unhappy rebellion' and exclaims: 'A great deal of innocent blood was shed. Good God, what a brute man becomes when ignorant and oppressed. Oh Liberty! What horrors are committed in thy name! May every virtuous revolutionist remember the horrors of Wexford!' O'Connell discerned from this [13] experience, which clearly affected him deeply, that it was essential to 'have no secrets in politics' and that 'it was strictly necessary to work within the limits of the law and constitution' (20, I, 205; 20, II, 99). Thus he condemned Robert Emmet's Dublin insurrection of 1803 and Emmet himself: 'A man who could coolly prepare so much bloodshed, so many murders — and such horrors of every kind has ceased to be an object of compassion' (I, 97).

O'Connell was called to the Irish Bar on 19 May 1798; he spent most of that year in Derrynane and went on his first legal circuit in 1799. He had arrived on 'the Grand Theatre' at a most critical time in Irish affairs and he was destined to bestride the stage like a Colossus.

2
'The Man of the People'

I have seen Ireland a Kingdom — I reproach myself
with having lived to behold her a Province ... I
have an ulterior object; it is the Repeal of the
Union, and the restoration to Old Ireland of her
independence ... I do not desire to restore such a
Parliament as she had before. No; the act of Restoration necessarily implies a Reformation ... Let them
delay Emancipation but yet a little while, and they
will find that they have roused the sleeping Lion of
Ireland .... till Ireland is herself again — a Nation.
Daniel O'Connell to aggregate meeting, June
1813 (quoted at *29*, I, 116).

1

'It is a curious thing enough', O'Connell once remarked
to his 'Boswell', O'Neill Daunt, 'that all the principles
of my subsequent political life are contained in my
very first speech.' O'Connell, as a young Catholic
barrister, played a leading part at a Catholic anti-
Union meeting in January 1800; this début in politics
is most significant. O'Connell, displaying the moral
courage that was to serve him so well, revolted against
the pro-Union Catholic politics of his family, led by
Hunting Cap, upon whose favour O'Connell's inheri-
tance depended. His speech to the Catholic meeting,
menaced as it was by Major Sirr's soldiers, was short
and for a first, nervous, effort effective. He declared,
rather dramatically, that he would prefer 'the re-enact-

ment of the Penal Code in all of its pristine horrors' to the Union and he appealed for Catholics to join [15] with the Protestant anti-Unionists in refusing 'to sell their country' or 'to abandon it, on account of the unfortunate animosities which the wretched temper of the times had produced'. The resolutions passed at the meeting, proposed by O'Connell, opposed the Union as it would extinguish 'liberty' and the 'independence' of the Irish parliament to which was ascribed the prosperity of the previous twenty years: 'I know that although exclusive advantages may be ambiguously held forth to the Irish Catholic to seduce him from the sacred duty which he owes his country', declared O'Connell, 'I know that the Catholics of Ireland still remember that they have a country, and that they will never accept of any advantages as a *sect* which would debase and destroy them as a *people*.'

O'Connell's entry into the political arena in 1800 on what became the primary issue of his political career — the right to self-government by the Irish people — raises important questions as to his motivation. His immediate self-interest would have been served by supporting the Union, which Catholics had been led to believe would bring Emancipation as well as opening up great prospects for a talented young Catholic barrister. This was Hunting Cap's outlook. His letter to O'Connell, after this political début, is a minor masterpiece of shrewd advice from a calculating Catholic. Hunting Cap pointed out that it was to the government that Catholics owed their 'favours' and not 'to the generous and spontaneous liberality of their countrymen' as he put it with ironic force to his naïve nephew. He greatly disapproved of young Daniel's action: 'I know you have a facility of disposition which exposes you to rather an incautious compliance with those you live in habits of friendship with . . .' and he added that 'popular applause' was

short-lived 'but the inconveniences may be serious
and lasting'. Hunting Cap's views weighed against
O'Connell's further political involvement for some
years (VIII, 3378, 3379).

Why had O'Connell taken the dangerous anti-
Union stance? He was influenced to a limited extent
by his Protestant fellow lawyers at the Irish Bar, most
of whom were anti-Union, but of greater significance
was his own idealism and independent thinking.
O'Connell's entry into politics was a victory for his
Enlightenment-based self-education of the 1790s over
the West Kerry pragmatic and survival mentality.
O'Connell, not for the last time in his long career, was
prepared to make personal sacrifices for his central
ideals.

He believed first and foremost, that 'a people' had
the right to self-government and that self-government
was the best form of government. O'Connell never
lost sight of his central objective — Irish self-government — but his experiences in the Irish legal and political crucible over the next twenty years so moulded
the young idealist that the pragmatic, Kerry side of
him increasingly became the means employed towards
the achievement of that end. The process made him
appear complex, enigmatic, even contradictory.
O'Connell's personality, however, was conditioned by
the Irish situation in the early nineteenth century:
'It is very difficult to separate O'Connell from the
circumstances in which he was born, and the state
of the country in which he has passed his life' (*11*, I,
12). Had circumstances been different the attractive
young patriot of 1800 would have matured in quite a
different way.

2

For his many parts on the public stage O'Connell
was superbly endowed. He had great physical pres-

ence, robust health, enormous vitality, and a melo-
dious voice, combined with great warmth and humour.
His extrovert behaviour and immense mental powers
marked him as a striking figure among his contemporaries whether in the law-court or on the political
platform. He acquired the most thorough self-discipline, except in financial matters, and his success was
achieved through intense application and hard work.

In the course of the two decades after the Union
O'Connell's outstanding part on the legal stage as
'The Counsellor' meshed in the public image with his
chief part on the political stage as 'The Man of the
People'. O'Connell became a folk hero with a stature
and impact without comparison in modern Irish
history. In 1800, O'Connell had made a good début
on the political stage. His speech against the Union
was to prove extremely valuable for the future leader
of Repeal sentiment as the Union gradually became
discredited among Catholics. However, it was his
experiences in the court-room which determined the
thrust and style of his contribution to Irish politics
until the end of his career. In the court-room one key
O'Connell 'persona' emerged: successful, self-confid-
ent, able, (indeed more able than most of his privileged
Protestant competitors), popular for his denunciation
of oppression, the 'Counsellor' who could use the legal
system, run by Protestants, for Catholic advantage
and make fun of it in the process. O'Connell's legal
experience was to transform him into a unique
political agitator who had the confidence necessary
for a new type of popular politics within the existing legal framework. After a couple of years' practice
O'Connell's obvious advantages as a lawyer emerged.

He chose the Munster circuit where his relations
and contacts were plentiful and he soon displayed
the audacity, command of ridicule, insight into human
nature (revealing his close and thorough knowledge of

the Irish people), and a shrewd manipulative ability in
[18] legal procedure which made him 'the best criminal
lawyer in Europe' (94, 249). Whatever about Europe
he was without match in Ireland and his great success
was won in the 'intolerably galling' conditions of the
Irish Bar (to use Lecky's apt phrase): all the paths to
progress were blocked for Catholics and were frequently in the hands of men of inferior ability, who
were pronounced bigots and anti-Catholics — men
like Lord Manners, Lord Norbury and William Saurin,
the Attorney-General. It was, as O'Faolain observes,
'a shambles of exploitation'.

O'Connell's achievements were hard won and he
gained an unrivalled insight into the operation of
Protestant control in Ireland and into the futility of
using violence and outrage against oppression; for
those he could not save violent protest ended on
the gallows or with transportation. For example, in
Limerick in January 1809, O'Connell fears 'it will be
a bloody week' when a Special Commission sat to try
cases involving violence; his fears are confirmed: 'The
assizes have commenced. This day was taken up with
the trials of two unfortunate clients of mine both of
whom were convicted on the clearest evidence and
will be executed tomorrow . . . they were fine young
men deserving of a better fate' (I, 228, 230). Another
example: in July 1815 when O'Connell was in Clare,
lamenting the fall of Napoleon, he was in the midst
of 'the bloodiest assizes ever known. No less than five
persons capitally convicted, four of them clients of
mine, one *certainly* innocent but he will be hanged.
God, God, how cruel, how wretchedly cruel!' (II,
562). O'Connell's attitude to the use of violence in
Ireland deserves greater respect than many contemporaries or later commentators gave it, for he
knew violent agitation inside out — standing for years,
often alone, between men accused of it and their

almost immediate hanging. He was aware of the economic causes of Whiteboyism and the necessity for the reform of the laws 'made by landlords' but, as he pointed out in a speech in December 1813, he believed that a domestic legislature 'instructed in the facts, and interested in the results' was the only hope of such a reform (*3*, II, 113–14).

By 1803, as a Catholic junior counsel, O'Connell was clearly a success but he still faced very serious difficulties as he reveals to his wife in August. 'I have been in Ennis since the day we parted. The business was not abundant there. I got into that town without a single shilling, and left it after paying all my expenses with three guineas and a half. In this damned town of Limerick they always treat me badly. The fact is I have no kind of connection here.' (I, 96). By December, however, he expected 'to clear a thousand pounds' in 1804 and he remarked to his wife 'Not a day passes without enlarging my professional expectations. It seems to be that I press forward for the first rank. This is *entirely* between ourselves . . .' (I, 109). His earnings at the Bar rose from over £200 in 1801 to nearly £4,000 in 1813. There was a depression after Waterloo which affected his income but during the 1820s he averaged about £5,000 a year in legal fees (*85*, 203; *98*, 38n). O'Connell began to revel in his long days at legal work. 'You know how I love the bustle of the courts' he remarks to his wife (I, 159). More importantly, he vastly increased his self-confidence '. . . Every case I have been concerned in one way or the other serves to increase my confidence *in myself*', he confides to his wife in March 1807 (I, 179). O'Connell was learning the techniques he was later to use with devastating effect on the political platform, as he reports to his wife in March 1808 from Limerick (in contrast to 1803):

I have been, love, extremely successful here. All my prisoners have been acquitted. The dock alone has produced me a small fortune. I had the County Court-house this day for near an hour in a roar of laughter at a witness whom I examined, the judge, jury and all the spectators. I have always remarked that nothing advances an Irish barrister more than the talent of ridicule. At present I am a little proud, darling, of my success in that line . . . (I, 201).

Thus in O'Connell's throwaway comments to his wife we get glimpses of his powers: in April 1813 he writes, 'Darling, I am just returned from making a *'famous Speech'* and making the jury weep and acquit a man for the sake of *his wife* and children' (I, 420).

Some of the famous cases in which he was involved include the Magee prosecution, 1813; the Bruce v. Grady libel action in Limerick, 1816; his demolition of a witness in a smuggling case in 1820; the trial of Scanlon in 'the Colleen Bawn' murder, 1820; the 1824 and 1825 Whiteboy trials for the murder of the Franks family; and the Doneraile Conspiracy, perhaps the most legendary.

In October 1829 it was charged that the peasantry around Doneraile, Co. Cork, were involved in a conspiracy against the landlords of the district. Four of the alleged conspirators were sentenced to death and O'Connell, as the only man who could save the prisoners, was summoned from Derrynane to defend the next four charged. He arrived dramatically in the court in Cork, having travelled all night, and his cross-examination of the prosecution witnesses resulted in the jury failing to reach a verdict. These four and fifteen other prisoners defended by O'Connell were acquitted and those previously convicted were reprieved. This was O'Connell's most famous triumph

as 'The Counsellor' and it has passed into Irish
literature through Canon Sheehan's romantic account [21]
in *Glenanaar: A Story of Irish Life*.

O'Connell was, as Lecky points out

> . . . an eminently sound and well-informed lawyer,
> excellently instructed in the theory as well as the
> practice of law; a consummate master of its evasive
> subtleties, and at the same time a man whose dis-
> passionate opinion on any legal question was
> entitled to great weight. Behind the noisier, more
> brilliant, and more popular aspects of his character
> this basis of solid attainments always remained
> (*35*, 6–7).

He became a popular folk-hero because of his success
in court. 'Within the folk-tradition O'Connell is never
forced to concede victory to his own or the people's
traditional foes – the oppressive landlord or magistrate, the treacherous Englishman, the perjuring
Peeler, the religious bigot or the grasping merchant.
Against such foes he invariably triumphs' (*72*, 33).

3

O'Connell's independence from his uncle's wishes
went further than opposition to Hunting Cap's pro-
Union stance. In 1802 Daniel secretly married his
penniless distant cousin Mary O'Connell. O'Connell
had courted Mary, in secret, for at least two years
prior to the marriage: in December 1800 he writes
to her as his 'future wife' declaring 'Mary, I shall
endeavour to merit your affection – the most constant
care, the most unremitting attention – the truest and
most affectionate delicacy – and the most unbounded
love. Such are the resolutions which I form, not in
the moments of enthusiasm or passion, but coolly,
seriously and soberly. These are the resolves of my
life . . .' (I, 34). Mary was one of eight children: her

father, a Protestant Tralee physician, had died while [22] the children were still young. Mary and her sisters were brought up as Catholics and her brothers as Protestants. Rearing the boys in the father's religion and the girls in the mother's was common in mixed marriages at this time. O'Connell kept his marriage secret for six months until he could put his case tactfully to Hunting Cap, who had wished him to marry an heiress.

His marriage to Mary lost him a great deal of Hunting Cap's estate when the old man finally died in 1825. From his marriage, however, O'Connell derived more than adequate compensation for his financial loss: this is clear from the letters exchanged between Daniel and Mary from 1800 until her death in 1836. It is confirmed by the course of Daniel's life after Mary died, for between 1836 and 1847 her absence is an important factor in understanding O'Connell's behaviour.

She was intelligent, perceptive and understanding and she and her children gave O'Connell enormous pride and support. Of eleven children seven lived to grow up: Maurice, 1803; Morgan, 1804; Ellen, 1805; Catherine, 1808; John, 1810; Elizabeth, 1810; and Daniel, 1816. Mary was crucial for O'Connell in being perhaps the only human being in whom he could confide, almost totally, his misgivings, vanities, triumphs and defeats. Mary was 'the best of all human selections' while she felt 'it would be quite impossible for any woman married to you not to be happy': so they wrote after eighteen years of marriage and the extremely serious failure to come to grips with O'Connell's huge financial difficulties (II, 806, 807).

The charge that O'Connell was sexually promiscuous has always provoked controversy. The correspondence between Mary and her husband is powerful evidence of O'Connell's fidelity and devotion to his wife but it would be naïve to argue this as conclusive. Given O'Connell's enemies, it seems more conclusive that no reliable evidence has ever been provided to support the belief that O'Connell was sexually immoral. In Irish folklore sexual prowess was always attributed to the hero and O'Connell is the principal folk-hero in modern Irish history; it seems that here lies the origin of the popular tradition concerning this charge. During the 1830s *The Times* and other political enemies of O'Connell in Britain attempted to blacken O'Connell through Ellen Courteney's accusations but, as Denis Gwynn revealed in 1930, there was no firm basis to her allegations. The propaganda must have damaged O'Connell, however, despite its failure to fix a permanent scandal on him.

O'Connell's income derived from landed property and from the Bar. In 1806 Hunting Cap, becoming somewhat reconciled to the reckless marriage, settled the hereditary property on O'Connell (but retained the income for his life) and later provided money for O'Connell to purchase some land. In 1811, two years after his father's death, O'Connell's gross rental amounted to £2,400; later this declined and his landed income in the early 1820s was 'a clear £1,000 a year' (*85*, 202). With his rising income at the Bar O'Connell would have been very comfortably situated were it not for his lavish lifestyle and, as Hunting Cap put it, 'the softness and facility' of his disposition. When O'Connell, in 1805, purchased No. 1 Westland Row, he 'said goodbye to solvency' as M. R. O'Connell aptly notes. In 1809 he purchased No. 30 Merrion Square (now No. 58) against Mary's wishes '. . . I wish to God you could get the house in the Square off your hands. . . . For God's sake, darling love, let me entreat of you to give up this house in the Square if it is in your power as I see no other way for you to get out of difficulties' (I, 259). His increasingly lavish [24] lifestyle and hunger for status drove him to live well beyond his means.

Already in 1804 he was moving away from the West Kerry lifestyle when he writes to Mary: 'Love, my business increases daily. I do fondly hope that the time is not distant when you shall have all the luxuries of life . . . you may rely on it that you shall have your lace before you . . .' Again, in 1807, he writes '. . . I am really getting a load of money. At this rate you shall soon have not only carriages but a country house. It is an infinite pleasure to me to succeed thus as it enables me to give my sweetest little woman all the luxuries of life' (I, 133, 182). Significantly in 1808, Mary writes to O'Connell as 'the most respectable of your family in every sense of the word, notwithstanding the grand connections . . .' (I, 208). O'Connell continued to enjoy his West Kerry intervals of rest but clearly Mary did not, preferring as she did the more sophisticated urban life.

O'Connell lost a great deal of money through giving loans: when O'Leary, a Killarney merchant, went bankrupt in 1815 it lost O'Connell about £8,000. He only survived by borrowing from his uncle Count O'Connell (borrowings later to become gifts). In 1817 his debts were probably more than £20,000 and they had reached 'a disastrous point' by the spring of 1822. Indebtedness led to a family separation designed to cut down the heavy expenses of the Merrion Square establishment. Mary went to France in 1822 with the younger children and later to Southampton and only returned in 1824. O'Connell remained, miserable, in Dublin, living as modestly as he could with his eldest son Maurice. This financial trouble, often acute to the point of despair, accompanied O'Connell's political career, at all times, but was especially critical during the Veto controversy and at the foundation of the Catholic Association.

O'Connell expected to have inherited Hunting Cap's bequest earlier in his career but his remarkable uncle lived until his ninety-seventh year. Until 1825 O'Connell struggled to pay off his huge debts 'by degrees' as he wrote to his wife in January 1823 '. . . I fear it will take another year to complete my *freedom*. . . . The fact is that I always looked to the resources to come from my Uncle Maurice's succession as the means of paying off, and I went in debt on that speculation. God forgive me if even I was ever so criminal as to wish for his death. I hope I have been in some measure punished for it . . .' (II, 991). Knowledge of this background adds tremendous force to his justification for the O'Connell Tribute of his later years:

> My claim is this. For more than twenty years before Emancipation, the burthen of the cause was thrown upon me. I had to arrange the meetings — to prepare the Resolutions — to furnish replies to the correspondence — to examine the case of each person complaining of practical grievances — to rouse the torpid — to animate the lukewarm — to control the violent and the inflammatory — to avoid the shoals and breakers of the law — to guard against multiplied treachery — and at all times to oppose at every peril the powerful and multitudinous enemies of the cause (*14*, 66—7).

O'Connell's sincere commitment to his political beliefs emerges from a study of his financial situation: he took a course for many years contrary to that which would serve his own immediate prospects. It emerges in smaller ways too — in 1823 O'Connell, financially embarrassed as he was, was paying the school fees of the Burke boys at Clongowes because their father was serving under Bolivar in the cause of

South American liberation. His national position [26] involved him in countless donations to charity as well as to the upkeep of appearances when he could ill afford either expenditure. But his resilience, energy and optimism triumphed over his adverse circumstances which were, admittedly, largely of his own creation. The final reckoning, at the cost of his children, came after O'Connell's death with the sale of the Merrion Square house and library. Maurice, his heir, was fortunate to retain Derrynane itself.

4

In November 1804, the leading Irish Catholics, under Lord Fingall, resolved to prepare the first Catholic petition for Emancipation since the Act of Union. O'Connell, now confident of his ability at the Bar, resolved to participate in Catholic politics (I, 123, 125). His idealism was daily buttressed by practical realities — the case for political and civil equality for Catholics with Protestants was reinforced by personal motivation. O'Connell could only become a senior counsel and advance his career if Emancipation was won. By previous concessions Catholics had gained important advances. The final disabilities related to the right to sit in parliament, without prejudice to Catholic religious beliefs, and the opening of state and judicial offices to Catholics on an equal basis with Protestants. After 1800 Catholic Emancipation meant the ending of the parliamentary oath which described the Catholic religion as 'superstitious' and 'idolatrous'. This oath alone prevented Catholics from becoming MPs although they had gained the vote and could, in law, stand for election. None did until O'Connell's dramatic decision in 1828. Also implied in Emancipation was the entry by Catholics to all offices on a basis of equality with Protestants:

this was the real prize for many Catholic activists. O'Connell stated that Catholics were excluded from [27] over 30,000 offices in parliament, corporations, law and the army and navy (*3*, I, 81).

Such an 'Emancipation' threatened, in a fundamental sense, the 'Protestant Constitution' which provided for a state church — the Established Church of England and Ireland — to guard the public conscience. Most Protestant politicians found it difficult to conceive of a state which did not profess a single well-defined religious conscience. The Constitution was thought to depend upon the notion of the organic union of church and state. The great theoretical problem was how to accommodate Catholics within the framework of the British or Protestant constitution: to upholders of that constitution the demands of the Church of Rome seemed to be intrinsically irreconcilable with its very essence. It was widely felt that Catholicism was destructive of civil liberty and intolerant, and even that Catholics were subversive with their 'double' allegiance to the universal monarchy of the pope and to their own 'proper' Hanoverian king.

The great practical problem was the resistance of the Protestant Establishment, especially the Protestant Ascendancy in Ireland, who saw 'Emancipation' as opening the flood-gates to a Catholic take-over of power. To overcome these problems and the popular 'no-popery' cry, pro-Emancipation politicians suggested certain 'safeguards' or 'securities' to accompany Catholic Emancipation. The most important of these was the 'Veto' — giving the government some form of control over the appointment of Catholic bishops and possibly of parish priests. Another was to institutionalise the state's claims on the loyalty of the Catholic clergy by provision of a state salary. In effect pro-Catholic Whigs wished to preserve the

constitution by giving Catholics a stake in its opera-
[28] tion. Such 'securities' did not appear as a serious
problem for the Catholic Church in Ireland: indeed
there is little doubt but that the Veto would have
been conceded as part of a political deal for Catholic
Emancipation within the first years after 1800. The
Roman Catholic leaders who supported the Union
had done so in confident expectation that it would
be followed by Emancipation but Pitt, the Prime
Minister, failed to carry his cabinet or to gain the
consent of George III on the question of Emancipation and he resigned. However, for many Catholics
who recognised the difficulty of carrying Catholic
Emancipation, a 'qualified Emancipation' remained
acceptable until the late 1820s.

When O'Connell became a member of the committee to prepare the Catholic petition to parliament
in 1804 there entered into Irish politics the most
decisive force against 'qualified Emancipation':
O'Connell placed the Catholic claims 'on the new
score of justice – of that justice which would emanci-
pate the Protestant in Spain and Portugal, the Christian
at Constantinople' (I, 178 n.1). O'Connell pursued
'unqualified Emancipation' because of his belief that
religious liberty was a right for all men: he rejected the
concept of 'toleration' or 'favours' extended on the
basis of good behaviour or with 'securities' (14, 22).
His whole life was dedicated to the proposition, which
the Protestant Establishment and many European
Catholics could not yet understand, that it was possible to combine the fullest civil liberty with the
utmost religious fidelity to the faith and doctrine
of the Catholic Church.

O'Connell was up against not only a massive
popular Protestant assumption of Catholic inferiority
generally (especially Irish Catholics) but he had to
face the ingrained Irish Catholic wish to accept con-

cessions through ministerial favour rather than popular and determined assertion of their rights. He was quickly at the centre of Catholic politics. In December 1804 he was one of five framing the Catholic petition: 'The fate of millions perhaps depends on my poor pen — at least so in my enthusiasm I say to myself and *to you* — But to you, *you alone*' he confides to his wife (I, 131). He was prepared to go to London with the petition, at the cost of lost legal fees, as he felt a 'feverish anxiety' about the success of the cause. To his great disappointment the petition was rejected for consideration in committee by both Lords and Commons in May 1805. Catholics felt very hopeful when their advocate Fox came into government in 1806 but he died in office after a few months and Catholic hopes were dashed yet again. The Napoleonic menace was much more important at Westminster and it was difficult for Catholics to pursue any fruitful course of action. Carrying Emancipation was a most arduous and daunting task for politicians in the face of popular bigotry and the European situation. Catholic hopes came to rest upon the Prince Regent who, when the time came for his influence on affairs in February 1811, was to betray the trust of Catholics.

When Irish Catholics met in 1807 O'Connell's more aggressive attitude was immediately evident: his speech in February 1807 combined a strong attack on the Union as a 'disastrous measure' with an attack on the government: 'The present administration had emancipated Negroes ... they should introduce a Clause in the Slave Bill to raise Catholics to the rank of Freemen' (*29*, I, 42–3). Opposing O'Connell's new policy of 'rough work' was the old Catholic leader John Keogh who argued for Catholics to maintain a 'dignified silence'. Grattan's prestige with Catholics, including O'Connell, was sufficient to dampen down

any bold protests and O'Connell suffered a temporary
[30] loss of popular support as 'the ever-changing and
changeable Barrister' (*29*, I, 48).

The lines of division were becoming increasingly
clear. In parliament the protagonists of Catholic
claims — Grattan, together with Plunkett and others
— were fighting for a 'qualified Emancipation' as were
the English Catholics and John Keogh's supporters in
Ireland. Against these were the O'Connellites, who
rejected Grattan's speech in the Commons in 1808 in
favour of accepting some 'safeguards'. O'Connell
managed to swing the Catholic Committee and the
bishops behind his policy. He denounced the 'safeguards' as a betrayal of Irish interests, and he played
on the popular feeling that the freedom of the
Catholic Church was the last remnant of national
independence. Frightened by the popular uproar,
the bishops, at a meeting in September, decided by
an overwhelming majority to reject the proposed
veto as 'inexpedient'.

This was a seminal development out of which was
to spring the peculiarly Irish form of popular political
agitation: a mass movement organised and supported
by middle-class leaders with the help and blessing of
the Catholic Church. The anti-Veto arguments were
grounded in the belief that the religious domain was
the last bastion of the Irish people untrammelled by
British rule. Therefore, it was essential to keep the
Catholic Church free from British influence if there
was to be a national regeneration; in effect O'Connell's
political activity forced the Catholic Church into
secular politics and determined the role it was to play
for many years. O'Connell brought the Catholic
Church from a position of acceptance of state payment and a state veto to a policy of open and defiant
repudiation of both measures. But it took him from
1808 to 1815 to do it and it cost him and the Eman-

cipation movement a most divisive and bitter split
which lasted almost ten years.

The years between 1809 and 1812 brought
O'Connell towards the mantle of national leadership:
the constant issue for him was not to accept Emancipation at the price of church control by the state
(the government strategy being to tame the Catholic
masses through influencing the priests). Indeed
O'Connell would have sacrificed existing Catholic
concessions if an Irish parliament was restored, as he
made clear at a meeting in September 1810 when
Dublin Corporation petitioned for Repeal of the Act
of Union: O'Connell was attempting to reconstruct a
self-governing Irish 'nation' which would include
Catholics, Protestants and Dissenters. With Grattan's
question to Irish Protestants in mind — 'whether we
shall be a Protestant settlement or an Irish nation?' —
O'Connell sought to unite Protestants and Catholics
to form such a 'nation'. He argued that separated
from each other Protestants, Catholics or Dissenters
could only be exploited; if they would unite as Irishmen they would succeed in liberating their country.
He sought for all Irish people to abandon 'the
madness of party and religious dissension'. This
speech gave O'Connell his first great lift in popularity.
The real cause of the Act of Union, he argued, was
the 'religious dissensions which the enemies of Ireland
have created . . . .'

The times were not conducive to O'Connell's
appeal for an undivided non-sectarian nationality
and he was forced, as leader of the Catholic movement for political and civil equality, to demand the
dismantling of the 'Orange' or Protestant monopoly
in Ireland. He had to struggle against the hesitancy
(and even the apathy) of aristocratic leaders of the
Irish Catholics but the underlying currents ran in his
favour: in the post-Union period there developed

among middle-class Irish Catholics a political ideology [32] imbued with what came, later, to be called 'liberalism'.[1] Perhaps the most representative of Irish Catholic 'ideologues' was Thomas Moore, but Denys Scully, aided by the Protestants William and Henry Parnell, ably developed the Catholic case for social and political equality. In the 1820s John MacHale, Bishop Doyle and Thomas Wyse further enunciated the chief tenets of this remarkable Irish liberal Catholicism. These writers outlined, created and selected political values and goals for Irish Catholics which were quite exceptional in terms of continental Catholicism.

In brief, Irish Catholics came to believe in achieving liberty through reconciliation with Protestants and with England under the British constitution: their ideas were largely derived from the British political tradition of the Whigs but they argued for the enlargement of the scope of the constitution which, through the Catholic Association, they effected in practice. O'Connell and his movement became convinced of the belief that society should and could be transformed in their interest: the liberal faith in progress through free institutions took strong hold of the O'Connellite generation. New methods of political action, a new faith in public opinion, as tools for the regeneration of the Irish people were the hallmarks of the Irish liberal Catholic movement as it developed under O'Connell. Thus through the pamphlets and writings of Irish liberal Catholics novel suggestions for popular pressure politics were made: as early as 1811 William Parnell, grandfather of Charles Stewart Parnell, wrote to Denys Scully with a scheme to 'call every nerve & sinew of the Catholic body into action by quarterly meetings of all the *Parishes* throughout Ireland'. It would be easy to call such meetings, to control the people and to give 'union to the Catholic body' by raising 'generally & annually a very small voluntary contribution, if only [33] a penny from each labourer, a shilling from each farmer & five from each gentleman'.[2] Parnell forecast, in a remarkable way, the strategy of the Catholic Association.

It is in this developing context that O'Connell operated when, in 1809, he began the long process of shaping political machinery in support of Irish political demands. In the Catholic Committee he proposed that they re-form as a permanent Catholic Committee: the difficulty was the Convention Act of 1793 which forbade the holding of any representative assembly of a political kind, other than parliament and corporate bodies. O'Connell's legal mind became fully exercised in framing resolutions and rules to keep his organisations within the law and still functioning. Not content with a permanent committee, O'Connell, as chairman, proposed that *permanent* local boards should be formed throughout the country similar to the central one in Dublin. Fagan, O'Connell's early biographer, notes that towards the end of 1810 the Catholic Committee 'opened new ground and became a Committee of Grievances' and that O'Connell was 'laying up abundant stores of political knowledge, and training his mind . . .' (*29*, I, 74—5).

In 1811 tussles with the law became inevitable as O'Connell, forcing the pace, sought to have Catholic delegates from the country meet in Dublin; despite the reluctance of the aristocratic and conservative Catholics, such as Lord French, and the arrest of six delegates for defying a proclamation, 150 delegates met in October 1811. In November O'Connell was involved in the state trials over the alleged breach of the Convention Act, winning the first round of this legal battle with the government. The Catholic

Committee was invaded by the police and O'Connell [34] masterminded the answers for Lord Fingall to Hare, the investigating magistrate. In 1812 the government secured a verdict of guilty against one of the arrested delegates and this ended, for the time being, the existence of the Catholic Committee as a delegated body but the Catholic Board was formed as a non-delegated body.

O'Connell was now thirty-seven years old and on the threshold of assuming leadership of the Catholics of Ireland. He had begun to see that his life was passing by without any immediate prospect of equality; the hope of the Regency had proved false for Catholics and O'Connell in July 1812 reflected:

> Twenty years, however, have passed away, and we are still slaves. My days — the blossom of my youth, and the flower of my manhood have been darkened by the dreariness of servitude. In this my native land — in the land of my sires — I am degraded without fault or crime, as an alien and an outcast (*3*, I, 185).

From 1811 onwards O'Connell had begun to pay close attention to building up his power base as he travelled the legal circuit. For example, in August 1811 he remained an extra day in Limerick to attend a Catholic meeting and he 'left them quite deter-mined' to support his policy (I, 342). Cork, Clare, Kerry and other southern counties were mobilised behind O'Connell's determined policy due chiefly to his direct personal contact with them when on circuit. A Cork Catholic, John Stack, writes to O'Connell in January 1812 with resolutions showing that 'we are determined to stand by you in every sense of the word' (I, 354). In 1812, a general elec-tion year in which pro-Catholic candidates gained over their anti-Catholic rivals, further meetings around the country enhanced O'Connell's popular reputation and the year was to end with the popular cry in support of 'The Man of the People' at a large meeting in Kilmainham when O'Connell placed his life at Ireland's service. In Limerick in 1812 O'Connell was publicly professing himself as an 'agitator' and taking a most professional pride in this role (*3*, I, 198). In the internal struggle with those who opposed his policy of 'unqualified Emancipation' O'Connell could bring the weight of provincial Catholic opinion to bear. This was to be decisive in the coming struggle.

In 1813 and 1814 there occurred the final split over the Veto which rent the Irish Catholic organisation in two for a decade. The trouble arose when Grattan proposed a Catholic Relief Bill in the Commons in 1813: this conceded the right to the government to exercise some form of control on Catholic appointments. Accepted by the English Catholic Board and by the Irish Catholic aristocrats, Grattan's bill was rejected by O'Connell and his followers. In 1814 Quarantotti, acting for the Pope (who was a captive of Napoleon), urged acceptance from Rome but O'Connell persuaded the Catholic Committee to reject the Roman advice and he carried the bishops with him. O'Connell's famous statement that he 'would as soon receive his politics from Constantinople as from Rome' drew the line between religious allegiance and political loyalties: 'I am sincerely a Catholic, but I am not a Papist. I deny the doctrine that the Pope has any temporal authority, directly or indirectly, in Ireland' (*31*, 115—18). The Catholic pro-Vetoists withdrew from the Committee.

O'Connell had become totally absorbed in the struggle. 'I actually *rave* upon those subjects', he had remarked to his wife, in August 1811, and in his speeches may be traced from this time a personal identification with the Irish cause, a conscious-

ness of pre-eminence and the direct emotional appeal
of the 'Man of the People'. He lectured his popular
audiences on Irish history, popularising his view of
the past in order to take the 'subdued demeanour and
almost crouching walk' out of his Catholic followers
by showing Ireland's former greatness and the qualities of her people.

O'Connell's success in ending acceptance by Irish
Catholic opinion of the Veto was but one event
thrusting O'Connell 'into the throne of leadership'
to use O'Faolain's phrase; the major impact of his
performance in the trials of the bookseller Fitzpatrick
and the journalist Magee focused popular opinion
on O'Connell's extraordinary personality. Both
Fitzpatrick and Magee were but whipping boys in
the government's strategy to put down 'sedition' with
'legal' oppression. John Magee, proprietor of the
Dublin Evening Post, was prosecuted by the government for publishing an alleged libel on the Duke of
Richmond's administration. He was tried and convicted in July 1813. As counsel for the defence
O'Connell delivered one of the most famous speeches
of his career. O'Connell confronted the government
strategy head on by ignoring the question of the guilt
or innocence of his clients and 'trying' the government instead. In the court-room O'Connell came face
to face with the men who governed Ireland — Saurin,
the Attorney-General and Peel, the Chief Secretary,
sitting beside the judges and other high officials. The
trial became a major publicity success for O'Connell.
Hunting Cap wrote to reprove O'Connell's verbal
excesses, observing that popular applause 'has ever
proved a very perishable commodity' (I, 449). In
O'Connell's case popular acclaim was more essential
and lasting than old Hunting Cap could comprehend.

O'Connell's performance at the trial of Magee is
perhaps his most famous at the Bar. It marks the

arrival of an Irish Catholic leader with the moral and physical courage, allied to the immense ability, neces- sary to demolish the Protestant monopoly in Ireland and yet to define how the new Catholic movement might be accommodated within the British constitution. After destroying Saurin and the government's policy O'Connell vindicates the Catholic cause:

> I ask, what is it we seek? What is it we incessantly and, if you please, clamorously petition for? Why, to be allowed to partake of the benefits of the constitution. We look to the participation in the constitution as our greatest political blessing. If we desired to destroy it, would we seek to share it? . . . this system cannot last: . . . the Catholic cause is on its *majestic march;* its progress is rapid and obvious . . . its success is just as certain as the return of tomorrow's sun . . . .

O'Connell swept the country in popular acclaim — meetings in Louth, Kilkenny, Kerry, Wexford, Galway, Cork, Limerick, Waterford and Drogheda were, in effect, pro-O'Connell assemblies. As Fagan observes, the Magee case 'caused a lasting and universal sensation throughout the country' (*29,* I, 98). In Cork, in particular, a 'democratic insurrection against aristocratic pretension' occurred. In effect, the O'Connellite anti-Vetoists routed the local well-to-do Vetoists in a public meeting which broke up before the howls of the people and for months the split animated the Cork Catholics (*29,* I, 109–12). Cork had become an O'Connell stronghold and was to play a vital part in funding and supporting his later campaigns.

By 1814–15 O'Connell was the acknowledged leader of the more popular wing of the Irish Catholic movement: the significance of his leadership is to be found in his creation of a popular consciousness of religious freedom and civil equality which prevented 'Emancipation' from becoming a mere concession of eligibility for place and office to well-to-do Catholics. The government suppressed the Catholic Board but from now on it would have to reckon with O'Connell as the popular representative of Irish Catholics.

O'Connell set the seal on his popularity in February 1815 when he shot John D'Esterre in a duel. D'Esterre, as an impoverished member of Dublin Corporation, had taken offence at a relatively minor aspersion of O'Connell who had referred to 'the beggarly Corporation': O'Connell was forced to stake his life, his legal and political career on his skill with the pistol against D'Esterre, who was a crack shot. O'Connell's victory was perceived, at a popular level amongst Catholics, as an act of public justice on the Orange faction. Both sides had seen, in Denys Scully's words, 'publicity' as 'the original end and purpose' of the duel. Scully wisely advised O'Connell to publish his side of the story 'with decision and dispatch' and this was done (VIII, 3392). O'Connell emerged from the attempt to kill or humiliate him more popular than ever. He went on to confirm his popular reputation by attacking Peel, the young Chief Secretary, and when Peel challenged him to a duel O'Connell was apprehended by the authorities on his way to the continent for the fight. O'Connell saw that 'the real value to poor Ireland is the very contest itself. There was never such a battle. Waterloo was nothing to it' (II, 585). Though he did everything he could to fight the duel, he was deprived of the 'glorious opportunity' (II, 588). The establishment might taunt him with his being apprehended easily but Irish Catholics could only admire their hero who dared confront the Chief Secretary in mortal combat. O'Connell was conscious of the power of such events for the Irish Catholic imagination.

O'Connell had secured the popular leadership and had brought the Catholic Church in behind his policy of 'unqualified Emancipation'. He was to find, however, the post-1815 years until the mid-1820s 'one of the most trying of his eventful life' (*3*, II, 242). He had paid an enormous price for making Emancipation a popular issue. The youthful expression of non-sectarian nationality became subsumed into a strong Catholic party spirit: in a sense, as Goldsmith said of Burke, O'Connell had 'narrowed his mind, and to party gave up what was meant for mankind'. At a dinner in honour of Thomas Moore in 1818 O'Connell regretted that he was 'a party man' but it was 'his misfortune, not his fault, to be so' as he belonged to 'the party of the oppressed and excluded' (*3*, II, 262). O'Connell never lost his feeling of optimism, indeed his joy, in his idealism centred upon the improvement of the human race. Tragically, however, he had been forced to become a sectarian figure to his contemporaries; he had to endure unparalleled abuse as a 'demagogue' and a 'ruffian' — even more tragically, the development of his own career had necessarily to increase the very sectarian dissensions he deplored. Out of this tragic situation and out of the stalemate in which he found himself after 1815 he fashioned into shape 'the people' as participants in the political process and sent them forth into a new era of democratic politics.

Between 1815 and 1823 O'Connell was casting around for some way to make progress: in the face of mounting apathy, '. . . the unfortunate man tried, literally, everything that the human mind could devise to stir his people' as O'Faolain observes. O'Connell, now known to English radicals, began to think in terms of parliamentary reform before Emancipation. His links with radicals in England were restrained due to the caution of upper-class

Catholics. However in 1817 there was some agitation [40] in favour of parliamentary reform in Cork and Dublin. O'Connell attended when a short-lived Reform Club was founded in Dublin and he supported universal suffrage, equal distribution of seats and annual parliaments. He visited London in 1817 and was not impressed by English politicians feeling 'how cruel the Penal Laws are which exclude me from a fair trial with men whom I *look on* as so much my inferiors . . .' (II, 700). O'Connell attempted to keep an Irish Catholic organisation going but the Veto split made it almost impossible and O'Connell was increasingly subject to personal financial pressures. Ultimately he became convinced that his popularity with the people must be turned to greater political point if pressure was to be created in support of 'unqualified Emancipation' and with this conviction he set about the creation of Irish democratic politics.

3
'A Bloodless Revolution'

It is one of the greatest triumphs recorded in history
— a bloodless revolution more extensive in its
operation than any other political change that
could take place. I say *political* to contrast it with
social changes which might break to pieces the
framework of society.

Daniel O'Connell to Edward Dwyer, The first
day of freedom! 14 April 1829 (IV, 1551)

1

Thomas Wyse, the first historian of the Catholic
Association, wrote of the 'natural apprehension' felt
by the Association's opponents as it was 'a body,
whose orbit and elements were not to be accurately
measured by any of the known laws of our constitution' (*25*, I, 1). The Catholic Association spearheaded
constitutional development, especially the process of
parliament becoming responsive to organised public
opinion. Oliver MacDonagh properly assesses
O'Connell as 'a pioneer, the first cartographer of an
unknown continent, that of mass constitutional
politics and pacific popular democracy' (*73*, 169).
O'Connell's new strategy emerged between May 1823
and February 1824 when his new organisation, the
Catholic Association, was a tiny body of men meeting
in Dublin. He had, as Lecky remarked, 'entered upon
the brilliant period of his life' (*35*, 56).

The origins of the new strategy must be sought in [42] the political situation as it was perceived by O'Connell and his colleagues in the early 1820s. O'Connell, in the years before 1823, was somewhat at a loss as to how to revitalise the Catholic agitation: his proposals and gestures had neither overcome the split amongst Irish Catholics nor helped very much their parliamentary prospects. In 1821 O'Connell cleverly attempted to use the King's visit to Ireland to demonstrate Catholic loyalty and to bring them under the constitution. He later recalled:

> The part of my political career which required most tact and judgment was the management of the Catholic body preparatory to and during the visit of George IV in Ireland. If I have any merit for the success of the Catholic cause, it is principally to be found in the mode in which I neutralised the most untoward events. . . . It was the most critical moment of my political life, and that in which I had the good fortune to be most successful (29, I, 273).

For some time after the visit, O'Connell wore a cap said to have been given him by the King (II, 921). He was much abused for his 'foot-licking idolatory' by radicals but he was attempting to combine all creeds on terms of equality under the Crown and constitution. What could Catholics expect if they had been seen to be less than enthusiastic for their monarch? Loyalty was not to be 'the peculiar prerogative of one sect' and O'Connell sincerely wished to have Emancipation carried without the appearance of a sectarian victory. However, the 'No Popery' forces prevented this. He rejoiced at the discomfiture of the Orange faction when the Lord Lieutenant, Wellesley, who aimed to restrict Orange privileges, was attacked in an Orange riot, revealing, O'Connell believed, the

Catholics as 'the only genuine loyalists'. He established a good relationship with Wellesley who made some changes in Dublin Castle favourable to Catholics. But Emancipation still eluded the unorganised and divided Catholics. Conciliation simply would not succeed.

The first new stimulant for O'Connell was the victory of Henry White in the Co. Dublin by-election of February 1823. Together with others subsequently active in the Association, O'Connell formed a committee and organised the freeholders behind White. The celebrated dinner party, at Glencullen, at which O'Connell and Sheil, the Vetoist, were reconciled and at which a new organisation was planned, took place on 8 February 1823. O'Connell was now forty-eight years of age while Sheil was only thirty-two. O'Connell suggested an organisation along the lines of William Parnell's letter of 1811 to Denys Scully; possibly Scully and O'Connell had already discussed the organisation of a popular national movement. However it was O'Connell's superb instinct for distilling the essentials of a political situation, together with his knowledge of the legal constraints and the potential for constitutional agitation, that created the new movement.

In April the Catholic question was again debated in parliament and this further stimulated Catholic action. The agricultural depression of the early 1820s and the widespread rural violence which accompanied the distress must have brought home to O'Connell the manifold grievances suffered by the people and the political potential inherent in the situation. In 1822 Kerry was put under the Insurrection Act; Whiteboyism was present in Iveragh in the winter of 1821–2 for the first time (II, 937, 944). In response to O'Connell's efforts an initial meeting of Catholics was held at Dempsey's Tavern, Sackville

Street and O'Connell's line was 'to take the strongest
[44] measures the law will allow to enforce our cause on
the attention of parliament (II, 1013). O'Connell
managed to get continuous Catholic meetings in train
and rules and regulations governing the Association
agreed: significantly the aim of the new Association
was 'to adopt all such legal and constitutional measures
as may be most useful to obtain Catholic emancipation'. Newspaper reporters were to be admitted and
the books of the Association would be 'always open
for inspection': very quickly the *Dublin Evening Mail*
dubbed the Association the 'Roman Catholic Parliament of Ireland' or the 'Popish Parliament'. Protestants
were admitted on the same basis as Catholics (II,
1023). In the year between May 1823 and May 1824
O'Connell developed his more advanced approach to
Irish agitation and devoted his energies to winning
sufficient support for his novel policy. During this
period the Association was a tiny body which barely
survived; often meetings had to be adjourned, as not
even the ten members necessary for the quorum
turned up. It was O'Connell's own faith in his new
strategy which ensured the survival and later, the
remarkable expansion of the organisation.

The first and most important element in O'Connell's
new strategy was to expand the range of issues, grievances and questions dealt with by the Catholic body
in Dublin: in the process he politicised every issue
and changed the nature of the demand for Emancipation from one seeking an equality of privilege for a
section of Catholics to a demand for the liberation of
the whole Catholic people from their grievances,
whether agrarian, judicial, religious, administrative or
political. In building a nationwide organisation he
used 'the power of common grievance'. The second
element in the new strategy was to provide a framework for the political action of the Catholic masses as

they responded to the publicising of their grievances. For this he turned to the Catholic Church. He had priests admitted as members without the payment of a subscription. A great boost to clerical involvement came with the publication of Dr Doyle's *Vindication of the Religious and Civil Principles of the Irish Catholics* in October 1823. O'Connell now added the third and final element of his new strategy: the Catholic Rent. Regular small contributions from the people crystallised his policy on issues and grievances and on the admission of Catholic priests and created an effective channel of communication for the national movement now emerging. Sheil told a meeting of the Association that he did not expect Emancipation from a change of views in the government but from 'such a mass of population' which 'possessed a power which must at last make its way and ultimately burst through the gates of the Constitution' (*huzzas*).[1]

No one knew, or had any experience of, a continuous and systematic mass political movement which encompassed a whole nation. The debates in the Association between late 1823 and March 1824 were mainly on questions of policy and strategy; in effect O'Connell was shaping the first mass Irish political party along democratic lines. In February 1824 O'Connell presented his seminal report on 'the best mode of raising a general Subscription throughout Ireland' to the Association. Copies of this report were shortly to be circulated, on a huge scale, around the country. He used population estimates to show that it would be possible to raise over £100,000 from Catholics but he would aim to collect 'at least the sum of £50,000' every year. 'How easy', he declared, 'if only one million paid one penny per month or one shilling per year.' The money was to be used to forward petitions 'not only on the subject of Catholic

Emancipation, but for the redress of all local or general grievances afflicting the Irish people' and to pay a parliamentary agent in London. It would also be used 'to procure legal redress for all such Catholics, assailed or injured by Orange violence, as are unable to obtain it for themselves' and to support 'a liberal and enlightened press'. O'Connell intended to give some of the money for the education of the poor and to help the Catholic clergy in 'erecting schools, building Catholic Churches, and erecting and furnishing dwelling-houses for the Clergy in the poorer parishes, and ameliorating in other respects the condition of the Catholic Clergy in Ireland'. He also wished to supply priests for Catholics in North America.

The appeal to the Catholic clergy was very marked. Education was one of the main issues which the Catholic Association used early in 1824 to secure the active support of priests. O'Connell met very considerable resistance to his new strategy from the moderate and cautious Catholics in the Association but he persevered, and, as Wyse observed, 'under the auspices of the Catholic Association' there evolved 'a great system of political education' which progressed 'with astonishing rapidity' (25, I, 257). In parliament Canning denounced the new organisation:

Self-elected — self-constructed — self-assembled — self-adjourned — acknowledging no superior — tolerating no equal — interfering in all stages with the administration of justice — denouncing publicly before trial individuals . . . menacing the free press with punishment, and openly declaring its intention to corrupt the part of it which it cannot intimidate — and lastly, for these and other purposes levying contributions on the people of Ireland . . . .[2]

Despite the suppression of such 'Unlawful Societies', O'Connell ended the exclusion of 'the people' from

the political process: he changed the people's view of
parliamentary politics as much as the parliamentarians' [47]
view of the people and public opinion.

2

In the process of creating an Irish public opinion
which demanded Emancipation the Catholic Association pioneered and experimented with most of the
elements which are essential to political democracy.
From the rent collection sprang a vast number of
political meetings at local level, extensive use of
publicity and local political clubs to fight parliamentary elections. The Rent was collected in two
phases: between March 1824 and March 1825 the
'Old Catholic Rent', as it came to be called, was
subscribed and after the suppression in 1825 of
the Catholic Association, O'Connell had the 'New
Catholic Rent' collected between 1826 and 1829.
During the first phase about £20,000 was collected.[3]
The New Catholic Rent brought in about £35,000,
the bulk of this being subscribed during 1828, the
year of the Clare election.[4]

The first effect of the Rent was that it ensured
the very survival and development of the Catholic
Association. The Rent involved the Catholic Church
in politics on a massive scale and related such issues
as education and the progress of the Catholic Church
to Emancipation in a direct fashion. It also allowed
the Dublin activists to direct the national agitation
through the control of the funds and they effectively
diffused their ideology to the newly mobilised public
by means of the Rent.

The first phase in the collection emphasised local
grievances but the second, building on the public
opinion created, concentrated on political activity
directly related to parliamentary elections, especially

the support of freeholders being punished by their
[48] landlords for their electoral 'revolt'. O'Connell's main
areas of support can be mapped, as we know in detail
how counties subscribed. The eight counties which
were strongest in support had five large urban
centres: Dublin, Waterford, Cork, Kilkenny, and
Galway; the other counties were Tipperary, Meath
and Louth. There is an obvious relationship between
O'Connell's circuit practice and the heartland of his
mass movement, Munster. He received relatively weak
support in the central counties of Leinster and consistently low support in most northern counties.
Ulster subscribed £1,837 compared with Leinster's
£7,043 and Munster's £6,571 during the first phase
of the Rent collection; Connaught subscribed even
less, £1,408. This pattern was repeated for the New
Catholic Rent. O'Connell's failure to penetrate Ulster
was more serious than Connaught: in Ulster there
existed a concentration of Protestants becoming
increasingly hostile to the Catholic movement. It is
not easy to see what he might have done to assuage
Ulster reaction had he realised the long-term con-
sequences of this cleavage. He was unaware of the
depth of popular Protestant support in Ulster for the
'Orange' faction which he condemned throughout
Ireland. He appeared to Protestants to think almost
automatically of the people of Ireland as the Catholic
people.

At the local level the Rent evoked a response from
two key social groups who formed an alliance under
the Association. The first consisted of townsmen who
were discontented with their economic conditions
and with their political status and position; they
easily absorbed the O'Connellite message. The second
was made up of the rural middle classes and the
priests. Very often leaders from the towns went out
to organise the surrounding rural parishes. The better-

off groups subscribed the bulk of the Rent and O'Connell's frequent urgings of the value of small subscriptions confirms what an analysis of the Rent reveals, that the 'poor man' was only sporadically involved.

The Rent was an obvious success: the basic structure which it evolved provided the backbone of O'Connell's further popular agitations. Immediately after Emancipation the country subscribed a National Testimonial to O'Connell which brought in possibly as much as £20,000. O'Connell gave up the Bar to concentrate exclusively on politics and further collections of the Tribute or Rent facilitated his later career.

3

The distinctive feature of modern democratic politics is the participation of a mass national public in the political system. O'Connell, during the 1820s, created a public opinion which became decisive in parliamentary elections and secured Emancipation. Essential to this novel creation was the extensive use of literary and oral means of political communication. The central vehicle of the Association was the newspaper. Newspapers carried reports of the proceedings of the Dublin organisation and of the meetings around the country; they were essential to such propaganda exercises as the education survey, the national census and the highlighting of Irish grievances, which the Association devised to win publicity and mass support. The press, especially editors F. W. Conway of the *Dublin Evening Post* and Michael Staunton of the *Morning Register,* aided the vast postal communication network by publicising significant letters, petitions and addresses to the people and by helping to deal with the enormous mail. As well as national and provincial papers, extensive use was made of pamphlets, placards, posters and hand bills. The Association built up an impressive distribution network which centred upon key local contacts, roughly half lay activists and half clerical.

Ballads were popular at this time of transition from an oral to a literate culture. O'Connell was symbolised in the ballads as the 'deliverer' who was long sought for in the Irish folk tradition; he replaced Napoleon, 'The Green Linnet', as a folk hero and became 'Erin's Green Linnet'. O'Connell was likened to Moses (*102,* 34):

> The bondage of the Israelites our Saviour he did see,
> He then commanded Moses for to go and set them free,
> And in the same we did remain suffering for our own
> Till God he sent O'Connell, for to free the Church of Rome.

At other times O'Connell was symbolised as 'the Kerry eagle' — an image of faith, courage and supreme power: 'the bright star of our nation', 'the Moses of Erin'. Another ballad, called 'Clare Encore' presented O'Connell as a new Brian Boru.

The speeches of O'Connell and Sheil set the tone of the political campaign and provided the arguments which others simply reiterated. It is hard to recapture the tremendous impact of the great meetings O'Connell invigorated. Wyse suggests, and he was in a position to judge, that a meeting was 'an epoch, which fills a great portion of the peasant's existence ...' and he noted that the speeches were 'read and read with the utmost assiduity, learned by heart, discussed and cited ...' (*25,* I, 240—41). O'Connell identified closely with his popular audiences. Duvergier de Hauranne, a French observer of O'Connell, wrote in 1826: 'O'Connell is of the people. He is a glass in which Ireland may see herself completely reflected;

or rather, he is Ireland himself. He has been compared to an inspired peasant'. O'Connell knew how to merge logical and emotional appeals to put his audience in a receptive frame of mind; de Hauranne again:

> You should see him with his cravat loose, and waistcoat unbuttoned, in a chapel in Munster. He boasts of the beauty of Ireland, the delights of her valleys . . . of the incontestable superiority of her inhabitants . . . . He lends an eloquent voice to the sentiments, the passions, and even to the prejudices of six millions . . . . That is all. Hence his extreme popularity, hence also his numerous contradictions and inconsistencies.

O'Connell's physical appearance was an inspiration, with the commanding presence and magnificent voice in public address. His style of oratory was extempore and conversational and he spoke with a directness and naturalness, laced with well-known slogans, quotations and catch-phrases, such as Byron's 'Hereditary bondsmen'. He repeated his political themes clearly and consistently: a remarkable repetition pervades his public oratory. O'Connell outlined to O'Neill Daunt his doctrine of 'reiteration', giving a good insight into his approach to political education:

> . . . incessant repetition is required to impress political truths upon the public mind. That which is but once or twice advanced may possibly strike for a moment, but will then pass away from public recollection. You must repeat the same lesson over and over again, if you hope to make a permanent impression. . . . Such has always been my practice. My object was to familiarise the whole people of Ireland with important political truths, and I could never have done this if I had not incessantly

repeated those truths. I have done so pretty successfully ... I have often been amused, when at public meetings men have got up and delivered my old political lessons in my presence, as if they were new discoveries worked out by their own ingenuity and research ... (*20*, I, 223—4).

O'Connell saw his moral force movement as pioneering the new path of modern political development: his constant phrase was that 'there was a moral electricity in the continuous expression of public opinion concentrated upon a single point, perfectly irresistible in its efficacy' (*20*, II, 172).

O'Connell used two fundamental arguments. The first derived from the principle of justice which appealed to the people and O'Connell could arouse their feelings by a recital of grievances. The second was grounded in political expediency and was addressed primarily to the government and public opinion in Britain: conciliation of Irish claims would enhance the British Empire and avoid the great risk of civil violence and possibly ultimate separation of Ireland from Britain.

A prominent theme in his speeches in the Emancipation campaign was the threat of civil war if Catholics were not emancipated. The most famous example of this was his 'Bolivar' speech in December 1824. O'Connell was a great admirer of Simon Bolivar, to whom he sent his son Morgan to help the fight for South American liberation. An essential aspect of O'Connell was his consciousness of 'the cause of liberty' throughout the world; in March 1820 he wrote of the South American struggle: 'One more land of liberty is a conquest over despotism and over legitimacy which they cannot afford. Let us push the victory as far as we can. ... Let us work for liberty abroad since powerful oppression in the upper classes and turbulent insubordination in the lower preclude the possibility of working for liberty with either at home' (II, 813A). Later that month he wrote of the liberal success in Spain: 'The complete revolution in Spain is so auspicious a circumstance that I hail it as the first of a series of events useful to human liberty and human happiness. . . . I enjoy this revolution as all the scoundrels of society enjoyed the battle of Waterloo' (II, 823). In September 1820, he wrote from Kerry to his wife on the constitutional changes in Portugal:

> Oh, darling, were you not delighted with the Portuguese revolution? It is coming home to our oppressors, and I am collecting health in these wilds to live to see Ireland free and independent. What is most consolatory is that all these great changes are taking place without bloodshed. Not one human life sacrificed, no plunder, no confiscation, nothing but what every honest man must approve of. Darling, it fills me *with hopes* (II, 858).

In 1824 O'Connell went as far as he could in 'veiled sedition' with the famous 'Bolivar' speech:

> Nations have . . . been driven mad by oppression. He hoped that Ireland would never be driven to resort to the system pursued by the Greeks and South Americans to obtain their rights . . . if that day should arrive — if she were driven mad by persecution he wished that a new Bolivar may be found — may arise and that the spirit of the Greeks and of the South Americans may animate the people of Ireland.[5]

Proceedings were initiated by the government against O'Connell but, in a rather farcical trial, he was acquitted when the reporter upon whose evidence the government depended ignominiously swore he had been asleep when the words were uttered. In his

'Bolivar' speech O'Connell was spelling out the right [54] to resistance if laws were abrogated — an impeccable Whig principle and bulwark of the Whig constitution since the days of Locke. He simply saw Bolivar as a nineteenth-century Washington and his admiration was absolutely genuine.

O'Connell's success naturally added to his popularity. Typically he used his triumph to reinforce the benefits of the British constitution, in defence of which he would 'squander the last drop of his blood' as he wished 'to brighten the link that bound Ireland to England . . .' O'Connell explained he was attached to that portion of the constitution known as 'the voice of the people'.[6]

4

The Catholic Association pioneered the widespread use of political meetings at parish, county, provincial and national level. This involved an impressive network of local leaders and committees. O'Connell's policy was to use petitions to parliament and 'grievance letters' to bring pressure to bear on parliament; the effect of this was to orient the people, on a vast scale, to national and parliamentary politics and to involve local activists in parliamentary elections. O'Connell's personal impact at local level — sailing down the river in a procession of fifty boats into Wexford, being drawn in triumph into Waterford, putting Bible missionaries to rout in Cork and having 'the mob' draw him in and about Tralee — was both dramatic and enduring. Based upon press reports, it may be estimated that at least half the parishes in Ireland had a political meeting during the Emancipation campaign; there were one hundred and thirteen major county meetings and eleven provincial meetings.

These figures alone confirm that O'Connell's major

achievement during the 1820s was the massive poli- tical mobilisation of the Irish people into constitutional politics. The parish meeting, as a mechanism for political recruitment and participation, was an original contribution made by the Catholic Association to the political modernisation process in Ireland: farmers, priests and townspeople became active, for the first time, in permanent local political clubs. A coherent national political programme was formulated by O'Connell and enthusiastically embraced in the resolutions passed at the local meetings.

A representative account of a parish meeting is found in a letter from Father Thomas Moylan, parish priest of Castletown, Co. Tipperary in November 1826. Moylan reported that his parish met in the parish chapel, 'in compliance with your wishes', to petition parliament for Emancipation and that there were 'upwards of 5,000 persons' in attendance.

> The chair having been taken by Fetham Watson, Esq., Garrykennedy, Revd. Mr. Therry, Nenagh, addressed the immense crowd: on his appearance loud cheering commenced and lasted for several minutes. He dwelt for more than an hour in a most humorous speech on the merits of emancipation; after which he explained the validity of the Treaty of Limerick and the perfidy of its violation. This address had a most powerful effect on the minds of his auditors.

Two other priests detailed to the crowd 'the grievances to which they were subject' and 'completely filled them with a spirit of enthusiasm not to be surpassed'. Father Moylan addressed them on the proselytism of the Kildare Place Schools: 'In the middle of my address I was pleasingly interrupted by several voices ... crying out that a child of theirs should *never, never, never,* be instructed in a Kildare Street or

similar school.' Moylan sent £1 to cover the publication of the resolutions in the *Weekly Register* and the
Dublin Evening Post. He sent £5 for the relief of 'the
poor forty shilling freeholders' and requested books
to take the census of his parish and paper for petitions to both Houses of Parliament.[7]

The parish priest or curate, the local secretary,
the churchwardens appointed specially in 1828, the
collectors of the Rent from 1824 and other local
activists formed a politicised nucleus in most parishes
and became the local cogs in O'Connell's political
machine, which functioned into the 1840s. At the
provincial meetings the Association put on a massive
show of public support with huge processions decked
with the symbolic green branches and festoons. At
Clonmel, for example, in 1828, according to Wyse,
there were over 50,000 people in the town and with
green branches covering every wall, festoons, arches
and other colourful decorations on every street it was
'a well-ordered, well-disciplined levy *en masse . . .*'
with men in green costumes and green cockades
giving the appearance of a 'national army' as they
paraded to the music of the bands (*25,* I, 245–6).

The Catholic Emancipation struggle had colour,
glamour and excitement which, for the first time,
gave ordinary people something political to cheer
about. It is easy to see how the ruling class became
convinced that a revolution was at hand, especially
when the electoral revolt of freeholders threatened to
give O'Connell mastery of the county representation.

At government level there were serious divisions
on the Emancipation issue. Within the Liverpool
ministry there was a majority, including Liverpool
and Peel, opposed to concession but a minority in
favour; in the Irish administration the Viceroys, Lord
Wellesley (1821–8) and Lord Anglesey were supporters of Emancipation, as was Plunkett, the

Attorney-General but Goulburn, the Chief Secretary and Gregory, the Under Secretary, were opponents, as was most of the Protestant Establishment.

These opponents inflicted a major setback on O'Connell in 1825 when they outlawed both the Catholic Association and all political associations of longer than fourteen days duration. In the same year O'Connell suffered another setback in terms of popular support when, on the suggestion of Plunkett and others, he gave his support to Sir Francis Burdett's Catholic Relief Bill which included two highly important 'wings' to make it rise through parliament: these were state payment of the clergy and the disenfranchisement of the forty-shilling freeholders. O'Connell spent between February and May 1825 in London lobbying for Catholic Emancipation; he suffered a considerable financial loss of about £3,000 (III, 1241) but learned a great deal about English politics.

The death of Hunting Cap in February 1825 enabled O'Connell to recover somewhat from his financial loss, as he now inherited Derrynane House and a third of his uncle's financial assets. He gave detailed evidence to select committees of both Houses on the state of Ireland while in London and his political manoeuvres that spring were but a foretaste of the great parliamentarian of the 1830s.

A storm of abuse and protest mounted against O'Connell, especially when the bill failed in the Lords, but as O'Faolain perceptively observes, 'never so much in his element than when in hot water, O'Connell was at his best and his worst back in Dublin' (40, 219). Quite simply he put his opponents to rout, using the techniques of the mob orator, which allowed him to cover a compromising negotiation position which would have been near fatal to a lesser leader. The attacks lasted for most of 1825;

as late as December he defeated the 'wingers', that is, those who were hostile to O'Connell for his having accepted the 'wings', at a popular meeting in Carlow (III, 1271). By early 1826 O'Connell had managed to recover his total control and had re-imposed unity on the Catholic movement.

O'Connell's anxiety for a settlement in 1825 was due to his perception of the increasing legal difficulties for his agitation and to his lack of awareness of the coming electoral 'revolt'. He was as yet unconvinced of the validity of the forty-shilling franchise as a weapon in the fight. While a genuine enthusiast for a wide franchise he always insisted that the voter should be free to exercise his franchise without fear of punishment by landlords. There were also attractive aspects of church reconstruction to be looked at when considering the benefits of state support. The remuneration of the Catholic clergy had long been a problem and was to remain so because of the voluntary support system. State payment, without a Veto on appointments, as proposed, would not, he believed, compromise the Church. Right through his career O'Connell's inclination was to take an 'instalment' when he could not get 'the whole', provided he was not yielding what he regarded as essential ground. This was a classic instance.

The suppression of the Catholic Association weakened O'Connell's organisation from March 1825 until the major events of the general election in June 1826; in particular there was no Rent collection in that period because of the legal fears held by O'Connell. With a feeling of having been duped, he was determined to re-organise his pressure group, as he wrote to his wife in May 1825: 'We must immediately form "the new Catholic Association", I have it all arranged. They shall not get one hour's respite from agitation, I promise you . . . I never was *up* to agitation till now'

(III, 1239). At fifty years of age O'Connell was forced to develop and expand the techniques of popular politics to make his brand of agitation irresistible.

The most significant product of the national campaign mounted by the Catholic Association was the development of Irish political consciousness, which was quickly measured in electoral terms. As early as October 1824 Goulburn had written to Peel that, 'It is not concealed that whenever an election shall take place the people will be placed in opposition to their landlords and such members only returned as shall please the Association' (56, 389). Goulburn's foreboding was correct: the 1826 general election saw a widespread and decisive shift in Irish parliamentary politics. Out of the thirty-two county constituencies about half were affected by the Emancipation struggle in an important way. The Association adopted a policy of not disturbing candidates who voted for Emancipation, whatever their politics; in 1828 this policy changed and the Association opposed the return of all government supporters. Because of the 1826 policy there were significant contests in only eight counties but these clearly showed the complete change in parliamentary elections which the Association had wrought.

In Armagh 'glorious Charles Brownlow', as O'Connell termed him, and Caulfield beat the Tories after Brownlow had declared for Emancipation. In Cavan there was the first post-Union election contest when Southwell for the Emancipationists forced a poll of eleven days. In Co. Dublin Henry White and Talbot defeated Hamilton, confirming the 1823 victory. Kilkenny, like Cavan, had the first contested election since the Union with a thirteen-day poll though Pierce Butler, like Southwell, was unsuccessful. In Louth, which again had the first contested election since 1800, Alexander Dawson, a comparatively small landowner, won a remarkable contest when there was a 'general defection of the tenants from their landlords' to support Dawson after the Catholic leaders had hurriedly developed a 'systematic organisation'; it was in Sheil's words 'a choice between the distress warrant and the Cross'. Monaghan also had the first contested election since 1800 in 1826 when Shirley and Westenra defeated Charles Powell Leslie. In Waterford, there occurred the most famous 1826 contest with Stuart's defeat of Beresford, symbol of the powerful Protestant Ascendancy, and where O'Connell was proposed as candidate — the first Roman Catholic to be nominated since the penal era — in order that he might speak at the hustings. In Co. Westmeath there was a notable contest when freeholders deserted the landlords to support the Emancipationist candidate. After the general election the relief money sent by the Catholic Association indicates those counties where there was widespread freeholder support for the Catholic cause: Louth, Monaghan, Waterford, Westmeath and Cavan were the principal recipients.

1826 is the great turning point in Irish popular politics. Sheil hardly exaggerated when he declared that Ireland 'has been to a certain extent revolutionised' and he forecast that the Catholic Association would in future be 'master of the representation of Ireland'.[8] Even Peel began to contemplate concession, writing in November 1826 to J. L. Foster who had experienced the crisis caused by Dawson's remarkable success at first hand, being a candidate, 'When I see it [Emancipation] inevitable I shall (taking due care to free my motives from suspicion) try to make the best terms for the future security of the Protestant' (98, 161). The Association supplied what had been lacking when previous expressions of 'the Catholic vote' had occurred — a national organisation and policy together with national financial support. Before the elections the Catholic leaders, especially O'Connell, did not really believe that they had created the first mass Irish political party or that the forty-shilling freeholders would be a reliable source of electoral support, due to landlord influence and control. There were simply no precedents for what occurred. 1826 marks a major advance towards the concept of general elections as confrontations between national parties on national issues rather than that of a series of local contests.

The development of the first Irish party system — especially the local party organisations which sprang up — was a key achievement of the Catholic Association. After 1826, these Liberal Clubs were organised in eighteen counties and many survived into the 1830s, 1840s and beyond: they must rank as O'Connell's most durable legacy to the people he led. He gave them the techniques to oppose landed influence and eventually to topple it. These local clubs, organised by the farmers, shopkeepers, priests, professional men and the gentry, familiarised the people with the modes and machinery of parliamentary politics; their work, moreover, did not cease in 1829, but was continued directly and many counties were well prepared for the post-1832 Reform Act years which marked a second stage in the growth of political parties in Ireland. The Irish electoral clubs pre-date their English equivalents which emerged only after 1832: '. . . Ireland afforded to England not mere theoretic instruction in the matter, but an actual visible example of the power of the Platform when backed by organisation of a complete and thorough character' (69, II, 3—4). Perhaps only the United States had a more advanced party organisation than O'Connell had in Ireland during the 1820s.

Louth, Waterford, Clare, Cork and Dublin were amongst the counties where definite political clubs emerged as a consequence of the 1826 general election. Significantly Clare established the County of Clare Liberal Club in March 1827 with James O'Gorman Mahon in the chair and Richard Scott as secretary. This Clare Club arose from a county meeting in March and it was encouraged to establish parochial clubs by O'Connell. Members of the Clare Liberal Club attended local meetings and endeavoured to deal with local grievances such as those relating to proselytism. At the quarterly meeting of the Clare Liberal Club in April 1828 it granted money for schools in five or six different parts of the county. Stress was put on the importance of the registry of the freeholders and, significantly, Daniel O'Connell was acclaimed as 'the founder of the Clare Liberal Club'.[9]

In 1828, the promotion of William Vesey Fitzgerald to Wellington's cabinet as President of the Board of Trade caused a by-election to be held in Clare. This gave the Association an opportunity to put into practice the new policy of total opposition to MPs supporting Wellington though they might be, like Fitzgerald, friends of the Catholic cause. Major MacNamara, a Protestant, was first asked to contest Fitzgerald, but on his refusal, O'Connell made the historic decision to stand himself. In June 1828, before he had decided on his own candidacy, O'Connell had sent an Address to the members of the County of Clare Liberal Club urging them to justify his pride in the Club on the occasion of the forthcoming election. The existence of the Clare Club for well over a year before the election and the leading role of the Club's activists such as O'Gorman Mahon, Thomas Steele and Richard Scott in organising the 1828 election undoubtedly paved the way for O'Connell's triumph.

O'Connell's national political machine immediately rolled into action in Clare. We can sense the tone of the campaign from the following placard which was posted all over Clare during the election:

> Who beat Bonaparte, by accident, without any merit of his own?
>
> WELLINGTON
>
> Who will beat Wellington, thro' his own merits, and by the justice of his cause?
>
> O'CONNELL
>
> Irishmen,
>
> If we beat the MINION of Wellington, in Clare, the Great Captain is himself defeated, and by whom?
>
> By the
>
> Great Catholic Leader,
>
> DANIEL O'CONNELL
>
> We tread the Land that bore us,
>
> Our Green Flag, flutters o'er us;
>
> The FRIEND we've tried is by our side,
>
> And the FOE we hate before us.
>
> July 1, 1828.[10]

As in Waterford in 1826 so in Clare in 1828: local sectarian feelings were aroused in support of the 'Great Catholic Leader' and Protestants were inevitably bound to interpret the propaganda in such a way as to be convinced that O'Connell was the epitome of sectarian demagogues. At the hustings O'Connell's supporters, helped by the priests, mobilised vast crowds to influence the voters in O'Connell's favour: the discipline and abstinence from drink among the assembled people was remarkable given the fever pitch of enthusiasm aroused by O'Connell. The result was 2,057 votes for O'Connell and 982 for Fitzgerald. Writing from Ennis after his humiliation Fitzgerald reported to Peel that he was happy the election was over '. . . All the great interests broke down, and the

desertion has been universal. Such a scene as we have
[64] had! Such a tremendous prospect as it opens to us!
. . . no man can contemplate without alarm what is to
follow in this wretched country' (*98*, 159).

The Clare election finally convinced Wellington
and Peel that Emancipation had to be conceded.
Wellington wrote to Peel in September 1828: 'I con-
fess that what has moved me has been the Monaghan,
the Louth, the Waterford, and the Clare elections.
I see clearly that we have to suffer here all the con-
sequences of a practical democratic reform in Parliament, if, we do not do something to remedy the evils
(*98*, 133). The Duke correctly saw that the Catholic
Association, with its increasing emphasis on reform,
could trigger a popular movement in Britain if it was
not conciliated very rapidly; in military terms what
he did was to beat a strategic retreat.

The Catholic Emancipation Act passed in April
1829 abolished the old oaths of allegiance, abjuration
and supremacy as qualifications for parliament and
'any office, franchise, or civil right' and it substituted
a new oath: Catholics were now obliged to swear
allegiance to the Crown in its Protestant succession
and to disavow the deposing power of the Pope as
well as his assumption of any temporal jurisdiction
in the United Kingdom. In effect the Act allowed
Catholics, with a clear conscience, to hold all civil and
military offices except the offices of Regent, Lord
Chancellor and Lord Lieutenant. Restrictions on the
Catholic Church left in force by the Act, such as the
prohibition on religious celebrations outside houses
or churches, were, in practice, ignored from the
outset. Accompanying the Act measures were passed
suppressing the Catholic Association and similar
organisations and the forty-shilling freehold franchise
was abolished and a £10 franchise established in its
place. As a believer in universal suffrage, O'Connell

was opposed to the removal of the forty-shilling franchise. He had been prepared in 1825 to see this franchise abolished as he did not believe that the forty-shilling freeholder could exercise the vote independently of the landlord. By 1829 he had seen the possibility of the freeholders exercising the vote according to their wishes when there existed a countervailing power to that of the landlord and thus he wished to retain the franchise. But he was unable to convince conservative Catholics of the necessity to fight on the issue and it was simply not practical politics to have Emancipation rejected because of the franchise question (IV, 1536).

The victory in Clare had produced a great surge forward in local electoral activity and at least another twelve or thirteen counties had formed Liberal Clubs. Many of these Clubs, with baronial and parish branches, were sophisticated and advanced political organisations. At an extraordinary meeting in August 1828 the Catholic Association called on all candidates for parliament to 'pledge' themselves publicly to oppose Wellington's and Peel's administration until unconditional Emancipation was granted, to try to repeal the Sub-Letting Act and to support parliamentary reform, particularly the extension of the franchise and shorter parliaments; candidates who refused these 'pledges' were to be opposed. In reaction Protestants formed local Brunswick Clubs which laid the basis of Tory party organisation in the coming decades.

When Emancipation was secure O'Connell's opinion in March 1829 was that 'the Liberal Clubs ought not to dissolve themselves' as he did not believe that they came within the act designed to suppress the Catholic Association (IV, 1531). Many of the local clubs, such as Waterford and Cork, officially dissolved in the spring of 1829, but, in practice, they continued

as News-Rooms or were quickly re-established as
[66] Independent Clubs. When in 1832 O'Connell called
for 'a parochial committee in each County' to fight
the general election and to collect the National Rent
he was, in effect, seeking the re-activation of the
1820s system of local and county clubs which had
marked time but not ceased to exist since 1829.[11]
The prospect of a reformed franchise and the system
of registration secured a widespread re-activation; in
1832 at least twenty-four constituencies possessed
clubs in the Repeal interest and eleven had Whig-
Liberal organisations. The Tories were similarly
organised in nine constituencies (*76,* 89). After
Clare Peel was perceptive:

> The real danger was in the peaceable and legitimate
> exercise of a franchise according to the will and
> conscience of the holder. In such an exercise of
> that franchise, not merely permitted but en-
> couraged and approved by constitutional law,
> was involved a revolution in the electoral system
> of Ireland — the transfer of political power, so far
> as it was connected with representation, from one
> party to another (*69,* II, 21).

5

O'Connell's policy of calculated brinkmanship had
brought victory: 'Can we any longer delay to do
something? Must not that *something* be either restraints in Ireland unknown in the ordinary practice
of the constitution or concession in some form or
other?' Wellington asked Peel in September 1828.
Neither was prepared to risk provoking rebellion
and so Emancipation was conceded, with bad grace,
through fear, rather than as an act of justice; the King
was in tears as he gave the Royal Assent after pressure

from Wellington: 'As I find the country would be left
without an administration, I have decided to yield my [67]
opinion to *that* which is considered by the Cabinet to
be for the immediate interests of the country . . . God
knows what pain it costs me to write these words', he
wrote Wellington in March 1829 (*98*, 163–4). To
teach O'Connell and Irish politicians that the threat
of violence was the way to force through an act of
justice was certainly a lesson Anglo-Irish relations
could have done without but, sadly, it was to be a
lesson much remembered in the course of future
agitations.

English radicals learned another vital lesson:
Thomas Attwood in May 1829 declared that

> The Duke of Wellington has taught us how to com-
> mand reform. By union, by organisation, by general
> contribution, by patriotic exertion, and by dis-
> cretion, keeping always within the law and the
> constitution. These are the elements of Reform.
> By the peaceful combination of means like these
> the Irish people have lately obtained a glorious and
> bloodless victory . . . (*98*, 174).

It was O'Connell who had taught them how to
'command reform' and it was O'Connell whom
Attwood consulted when he launched his Birmingham
Political Union in December 1829. The Reform Act
of 1832 was obtained under pressure from powerful,
extra-parliamentary political association and with
O'Connell's help in the House of Commons. Well
might O'Connell exclaim in March 1829: 'How
mistaken men are who suppose that the history of
the world will be over as soon as we are emancipated!
Oh, *that* will be the time to *commence* the struggle
for popular rights' (IV, 1536).

4
'Justice or Repeal'

Oh Erin! Shall it e'er be mine
To right thy wrongs in battle line,
To raise my victor head, and see,
Thy hills, thy dales, thy people free?
That glance of bliss is all I crave
Between my labours and the grave.
    quoted by O'Connell to O'Neill Daunt (*20*, II, 8)

1

The course O'Connell adopted after the great triumph
of 1829 forms the turning point of his career. He was
later to write that he had

> ... dreamed a day dream — *was* it a dream? — that
> Ireland still wanted me, that although the Catholic
> aristocracy and gentry of Ireland had obtained
> most valuable advantages from Emancipation, yet
> the benefits of good government had not reached
> the great mass of the Irish people, and could not
> reach them unless the Union should be either made
> a reality — or unless that hideous measure should
> be abrogated (*14*, 68).

In March 1829 Irish Catholics began to collect a
national testimonial for O'Connell as a mark of
gratitude for his services to Emancipation. O'Connell
believed that this would finally free him from debt
and enable him to pay his daughters' fortunes (IV,

1557). During the year O'Connell received possibly as much as £20,000 in this remarkable national gesture by Catholics. It confirmed O'Connell in his growing self-identification with the cause of Ireland. From 1830 an O'Connell Tribute was collected annually in support of his political efforts and in the best years he received over £16,000, but it varied with the ebb and flow of his popularity. The income, in Greville's phrase, was an 'income nobly given and nobly earned' and it was essential to O'Connell's independence, as the clumsy attempt by Whigs to buy him off in December 1830 proved (*76*, 21). To understand O'Connell fully in the final seventeen years of his life it is necessary to appreciate his legal and political labours during the Emancipation campaign of the 1820s.

O'Connell had devoted himself relentlessly to his legal practice and to the Catholic struggle. In 1822 he wrote to his wife 'My *trade* goes on flourishingly. All the rest of the Bar are complaining but I never was doing so much. In your absence I have nothing to take up a moment of my time but law. I rise at half after four, breakfast at ¼ after eight, dine at a quarter after five and go to bed between nine and ten' (II, 962). Again in January 1824 he writes:

> How monotonous my life is. The history of one day is the story of all. I rose today at soon after five. I worked till a quarter after eight by the town. Then breakfast. I eat two fresh eggs every day which is making me fat. Working then till a quarter before eleven. Then to Court. There until near four. At four on my way home call at Milliken's, (bookseller) read the morning papers *for nothing,* then home . . . so work until a quarter after five by the town. Then dine. In my study again before half after six . . . so work till this hour, half after nine (III, 1081).

This punishing legal schedule, together with his
political exertions as a middle-aged man, affected his physical appearance: 'I do not take any wine or punch and yet I am growing more and more corpulent. I do not know, darling, what to do with myself to keep this propensity in order. I rise early, keep on my legs and walk very fast through the streets. Yet I get fat. I ought not, I believe, to eat so much . . .' (III, 1096). O'Connell longed to be free of the tedious and relatively unrewarding legal work of a junior counsel, yet in 1829 he was passed over in legal preferment when Sheil and other barristers with less ability were made King's Counsel. He was faced with a continuation of his exhausting legal practice had he not committed himself totally to politics. Even in 1834 O'Connell reflected that had he retired from politics he would have 'sunk into a mere professional drudge' (V, 2121).

To all his political instincts was added the pressure of popular expectation after his great victory. O'Connell well knew that he had the support of the people, not because of his explicit political principles, but because he was 'a fellow Catholic and a man long the theme of *ballads* and conversation' as he remarked to Jeremy Bentham; he was, he knew, 'identified with the peasantry by the community of religion and exclusion' (VIII, 3409). There was a deep feeling in O'Connell that he had a mission for these people, that he had 'helped to *convert* the people of Ireland from apathy, despair and from nocturnal rebellion into determined but sober politicians' (VIII, 3410). He felt responsible for and to the Irish people and this, the inevitable price of his unparalleled popular leadership, predetermined his last tragic years. O'Connell was snubbed in England, and by English Catholics as well; he was forced to be re-elected in Clare due to the vindictiveness of the government and he considered the government quite despotic, with their suppression of political associa- tions, the disenfranchisement of the freeholders and the recall of Anglesey, the liberal-minded Viceroy. His acquaintance with the House of Commons and his speech at the bar of the House in May 1829 confirmed his own belief that he would be successful in a parliamentary career, even at fifty-five years of age. These were some of the factors O'Connell had in mind when he committed himself to a new career of agitation in 1829. However, it was his view of himself in relation to the Irish people, together with his political beliefs, that was decisive in this commitment.

To grasp adequately O'Connell's political beliefs it is essential to understand the school of thought known as Philosophical Radicalism. The leaders of the Radicals were Jeremy Bentham (1748–1832) and James Mill (1773–1836). Their basic doctrine was the 'principle of utility', or 'greatest happiness' principle. Bentham had elaborated the doctrine, at great length, in his *Introduction to the Principles of Morals and Legislation* (1789). The 'principle of utility' was a means of measuring actions according to the tendency which each action appeared to have for increasing or diminishing happiness. Philosophical Radicals believed that this was the governing principle of both private and public conduct and the only sound basis of policy. They assumed that the sole motive of men was self-interest and that each man was the best judge of his own interests. These early radicals restricted the function of parliament largely to the removal of restrictions on the free action of individuals, unless a measure was clearly needed to ensure such freedom. They did not see 'society' as an organism but concentrated on the individual: if each person acted rationally by seeking his own self-interest the total result would be 'the greatest happiness of the greatest number'.

O'Connell was heir to the principles of the Whig
Revolution, first clearly stated by Locke, and em-
bodied in the great political manifestos of the
American and French Revolutions: such general
liberties as freedom of thought, of expression, of
association, the security of property and the control
of parliament by an informed public opinion seemed
to liberals, like O'Connell, certain of progressive and
universal realisation. At the core of this mode of
political thought was a fundamental belief that all
value inheres ultimately in the satisfactions and the
realisations of the human individual. O'Connell came
to believe, as did many liberals and radicals, that as
he was riding the tide of history, evolutionary changes
rather than revolutionary violence would establish
civil and political liberty. The ideals of liberalism
were an aftermath of the revolutionary era but its
achievements were to be, largely, the outcome of a
utilitarian and practical application of these principles
to specific problems.

If it appears now that Philosophical Radicalism was
largely an ideology for middle-class interests, to
O'Connell and his radical contemporaries it was a
philosophy for a national community whose ideal
would be to protect and conserve the interests of all
classes. They were sincere and public-spirited men but
their emphasis on the individual frequently led them
to regard communal interest groups and mass organisations as reactionary and anti-liberal.

O'Connell looked forward to being Bentham's
'mouthpiece' in parliament. He obviously owed much
of his parliamentary programme to his Benthamite
leanings. O'Connell was an avid reader of the newly
founded radical *Westminster Review* and helped to
circulate it in Ireland (VIII, 3416). In July 1828
Bentham evidently invited O'Connell to visit him
but O'Connell replied that he was unable 'to leave

Ireland even for the purpose of replenishing myself
with the reasons of that political faith which is in
me'. He regretted that he could not devote the rest
of his life to the cause of 'the greatest possible good
to the greatest possible number' as he could only
'dedicate to political subjects as much time as can be
torn from my profession' (VIII, 3404). After his
Emancipation victory he outlined to both English
and Irish audiences his political opinions and aims.
He announced to a meeting of Westminster electors,
with Cobbett, that he was 'a reformer, a radical
reformer' and he issued to the Clare electors his
famous 'Address of the Hundred Promises' pledging
himself to secure a wide variety of reforms.[1] In the
House of Commons in March 1830 O'Connell boasted
of belonging to 'the small and sacred band of Radical
Reformers'.[2] Here was the public emergence of
O'Connell, the radical reformer, who had previously
subordinated his radicalism to the conservative ethos
of the Irish Catholic struggle.

However, it would be a gross oversimplification to
describe O'Connell simply as a Benthamite radical. He
was first and foremost, in 1829, a popular leader with
a position unparalleled in Europe. Advantage to the
Irish people was always his first priority. Significantly,
he told Bentham that the Irish hated J. R. McCulloch,
the Scottish laissez-faire economist, because McCulloch
advocated the view that absenteeism was not a major
cause of Irish agrarian ills and because he supported
the Sub-Letting Act which had 'murdered' thousands
through land clearances (VIII, 3417). O'Connell was,
next, a very rare sort of Catholic liberal deriving
inspiration in equal measure from both his Catholicism
and his liberalism:

I belong to a religion which teaches the merits of
good works; and I am quite sincere votary of that

creed. Besides the pleasure of doing good, and the gratification which a light heart feels even at the attempt to be useful, there is — I hope I say it without any tinge of hypocrisy — a higher propelling motive on my mind. There is the stimulant, I hope, of religious duty and spiritual reward. There are many who would smile at my simplicity — and the *liberaux* of France who hate religion much more than they do tyranny — would sneer at me. Yet it is true. I do look for a reward exceedingly great for endeavouring to terminate a system of fraud, perjury, and oppression of the poor.

Thus O'Connell explained his motivation to Bentham in October 1828 (VIII, 3408). He was acutely aware of how his liberalism differed from continental liberalism which seemed to oppose religion, especially Catholicism (*14,* 104). He offered his parliamentary services to the Catholic bishops of Ireland in 1829 (IV, 1597; VIII, 3414) and he turned his thoughts in June 1829, as he told Pierce Mahony, 'exclusively to what I deem useful to Ireland', declaring that he was 'thoroughly convinced that nothing but "the Repeal of the Union" can permanently serve her interests' (IV, 1581).

O'Connell was always prepared to regard the question of Repeal not as an absolute necessity but as the most likely means of achieving justice and good government for the Irish people. He knew better than most that he had no chance of parliamentary success in his argument for Repeal but he also knew he might convince the Whigs to conciliate Repeal sentiment in Ireland. As for actually securing Repeal, he had in the course of his life seen changes which no one had foreseen: all things were to be hoped for in that revolutionary age. He accepted the radical programme *tout court* save where there was a clear political advantage to his Irish followers in opposing it.

O'Connell did not work out a well-defined social or economic programme; indeed his ultimate strength lay in his ability to put forward vigorously the ill-defined demand of the Irish people for justice and good, representative government. He believed that he led a new movement in history, 'the party of the bloodless movement', which respected both the sacred and the secular:

> My conviction thoroughly is that the real liberal party — the peaceful movement party — is that which alone can produce salutary results to men, and also that it most conduces to the good of religion, and the just independence of the Catholic Church . . . I cherish it (the party) as the best hope of rational freedom. I cherish it because I am the friend of perfect liberty to every man of every colour, caste, and creed throughout the world. (*14*, 103).

2

During the 1820s O'Connell's family began to be significant in his political efforts. His second son, Morgan, a lively and cheerful young man, enlisted, before he was sixteen, as an officer in the Irish legion recruited to aid Bolivar in South America. Morgan's part was well publicised and gave O'Connell a certain 'aura' within Irish politics: he just might be the man to imitate Bolivar. O'Connell refused to allow Morgan to join the British army; he eventually joined the Austrian army. He returned to Ireland to become part of O'Connell's 'tail' as an MP in 1832 but he had little real interest in politics. Maurice, the eldest son, a barrister, was extremely lazy; he took some part in the Catholic Association and O'Connell had him elected MP in 1831; he supported his father until

O'Connell's death in 1847. In 1825, O'Connell's
[76] eldest daughter, Ellen, married Christopher FitzSimon,
a small Catholic landlord who became an MP in 1832
as a Repealer supporting O'Connell. The younger
children remained a source of pride to the aging
O'Connell: John, the third son, showed more interest
in politics than the others and O'Connell had him
elected MP in 1832 in his early twenties; he was to
play a significant role in the last years of his father's
life as a leader in the Repeal Association. O'Connell
bought a partnership for his youngest son Daniel in
a new brewery in Dublin but he did not prosper and
ended his connection with the firm in 1841. He
became MP for Dundalk in 1846 and later settled
in England.

O'Connell's children lacked their father's energy and
ambition and also his outstanding ability. They were
brought up by their mother and due to O'Connell's
lengthy and frequent absences were probably more
influenced by her. In 1824, when O'Connell was
considering where to re-unite his separated family,
Mary O'Connell argued that Ellen and Kate 'would
rather live in the greatest obscurity anywhere than
live in any of the country parts of Ireland' obviously
being influenced by Mary's arguments that 'country
society' would be disadvantageous to girls 'educated
as they have been' (III, 1087). Mary's social ambitions emerge in her correspondence, as in 1826 when
she feels snubbed by Dublin Castle society and
O'Connell resorts to promising her an invitation to
a state dinner: 'What a grand little woman you will be
then . . .' (III, 1301). Though O'Connell refurbished
Derrynane House after 1825 and clearly revelled in
the weeks he spent there, his West Kerry pleasures
were not shared by his wife or children. The tremendous O'Connell life-force displayed by Hunting Cap
and Daniel O'Connell was not transmitted through

Mary O'Connell to the next generation which was characterised by bourgeois mediocrity.

3

O'Connell's political efforts from 1830 to his death in 1847 were on a larger stage than before Emancipation. He began to operate, in a highly sophisticated fashion, at a number of diverse levels: in the House of Commons as an outstanding parliamentarian; in Ireland building the first Irish political party and the local political machinery; channelling the great popular agitation of the 'Tithe War' in Ireland; beginning to play a significant role in liberal, radical and humanitarian movements in Britain, Europe and America. There were connections between all these 'O'Connells' but it is easy to understand how contemporaries, from whatever vantage point, sometimes failed to appreciate his efforts. Never before, and certainly never since, has an Irish popular leader been so devoted to Irish politics while also making a world-wide impact on the great causes of his time. His work in the 1830s has been misunderstood, especially in Ireland, but it was during that decade that O'Connell displayed his parliamentary genius and in so doing first made Irish issues central to British politics.

'I am fast learning the tone and temper of the House' O'Connell wrote within days of entering the Commons in February 1830 (IV, 1637); his maiden speech announced him as 'the member for Ireland', as Cobbett called him. O'Connell told the House that the Irish people 'had sent him thither to do the work of the people' and that he represented Irish wants, wishes and grievances.[3] His unique position as the Catholic Irish representative who had forced his way into parliament at the age of fifty-five by means that were hated and feared soon involved him in controversy. As Oliver MacDonagh observes, O'Connell [78] 'had ranged against him the peculiar combination of insolence and frightened ruthlessness which marks a privileged order under threat' (72, 43); he became, as Lecky noted, 'a kind of pariah' in English society and was kept at a distance by the English parties.

Ingrained prejudice against the Irish Catholics and imperialistic selfishness soon had O'Connell reacting with 'his old Association style' to hostile receptions in the Commons (IV, 7222). In November 1830 he attacked the ministerial benches thus: 'Ye place-holders, who revel on the hard earnings of the people, ye pensioners who subsist on the public money; ye tax-consumers and tax-devourers, assault me as you please. I am not to be intimidated by you. I shall continue to stand by Ireland, for I represent her wants, her wishes, and her grievances.'[4]

O'Connell became extremely active in the Commons: he immediately sought to bring in a Reform bill, he opposed West Indian slavery, the monopoly of the East India Company, Jewish disabilities, game laws, the blasphemy laws and flogging in the army. He supported law reform, free trade, reduction of the National Debt, universal suffrage and the liberal cause in Europe and the colonies. His speeches, laced with ironical allusions and scathing remarks, but demonstrating his range of interests and grasp of facts and issues, won him the reluctant admiration and ear of the Commons. O'Connell's March 1831 speech on parliamentary reform was praised even by *The Times* which, however, soon became his chief opponent in the English press and indulged in the most abusive anti-O'Connell remarks published in England.

O'Connell's parliamentary achievements during the 1830s included his major part in the passage of the Reform Act of 1832 and in the abolition of slavery but also his support for the whole course of liberal legislation which profoundly modified social and administrative structures during the decade. His achievements in holding the balance of power and keeping the Melbourne government in power over several sessions of parliament was the result of his creation and leadership of the first modern political party in the Commons.

In January 1830 O'Connell's 'Letter to the People of Ireland' put forward a comprehensive political programme which included Repeal, parliamentary reform, law reform, some plan for the provision of the aged and destitute poor (he suggested a 20 per cent tax on the incomes of absentees for the poor), abolition of tithes, administrative reform, repeal of the Sub-Letting Act, changes in the Vestry Act, reform of Grand Juries and municipal reform (*29, II, 24–30*). He was faced with a difficult tactical position if he was to achieve any part of his programme between 1830 and 1832. The wave of revolutions in Europe in 1830, while a reason for hope to him, were for both Whigs and Tories solid justifications for repressing O'Connell in Ireland: the Irish government in 1830 acted as if it had to deal with a potentially revolutionary situation and it was determined to crush O'Connell's organisations.

O'Connell fought the general elections of July-August 1830 and April-May 1831 on a broad anti-Tory front. Despite Whig repression after November 1830 when they came to power, it mattered deeply to O'Connell that the Whigs rather than the Tories were in power. To the Whigs he might look for reform and through the Commons gain 'something for Ireland'; from the Tories he expected not only repression but that the power of the state would be thrown behind the Protestant 'faction' in Ireland. O'Connell and Peel had for many years loathed and despised each other. O'Connell's major drive during [80] the 1830s aimed to loosen the grip of the Protestant 'faction' in Irish affairs: in February 1833 he could point out in the House of Commons, four years after Catholic Emancipation, that there was not in Ireland a single Catholic judge or stipendiary magistrate, that all the high sheriffs, with one exception, and the overwhelming majority of the unpaid magistrates and of the grand jurors, the five inspectors-general and the thirty-two inspectors of police were Protestants. He also pointed out that the chief towns were in the hands of narrow, corrupt, and for the most part, intensely bigoted corporations.[5]

Through his Whig alliance O'Connell achieved a loosening of the grip, giving 'a brain-blow to the Orange faction' (V, 2228); his Irish achievement during the 1830s was to produce a lasting shift in power and influence at both local and national level. That shift commenced in earnest in 1830 and 1831 when the elections destroyed the long-standing Tory majority in the Irish representation (76, 15). O'Connell gave a virtuoso demonstration in political improvisation when combating repression by forming new associations, holding 'private' breakfasts, calling for a run on the banks and doing the rounds of meetings in the country to keep 'the machine in regular and supple motion' (IV, 1716). This performance culminated in his arrest in January 1831 together with seven associates on thirty-one charges of conspiracy, seditious libel and unlawful assembly.

The Whigs had attempted to bribe O'Connell with office in December 1830; O'Connell was offered a judgeship or Mastership of the Irish Rolls (76, 21). O'Connell was 'not to be had', however. Now they attempted to destroy him. It is easy to get an idea of the virulence against O'Connell in Stanley's note to Melbourne, quoting the attorney-general Blackburne who had said, 'I now give him bound hand and foot into your custody — don't let him go'. Stanley added '. . . I think he may be dealt with — *and transported* — and if he were, I really hope Ireland would be tranquil' (*76*, 23). The Whigs, however they despised and feared O'Connell, needed him for the passing of Reform. The case dragged until May and ended, in reality, in a victory for O'Connell, though at what psychological cost is hard to say. O'Connell believed that Ireland's prospects would be greatly improved in a reformed parliament so he gave his vital support and instituted the National Political Union to bring together all Irish reformers and to facilitate support for the Whigs in parliament.

In reading O'Connell in *Hansard* it is easy to see the problem he presented to opponents and admirers alike: his most frustrating characteristic was his combination of radical political ideals and espousal of Repeal of the Union with expedient acceptance of half-measures and substitutes or whatever was the best offer available to advance his cause. Moreover O'Connell never hesitated to use the most appropriate argument at any given moment to gain the advantage with little regard for consistency in reasoning his case. In 1831, for example, he told the House that 'the object of those who advocated Repeal of the Union was to obtain cheap government and a just administration of the laws. . . . The Repeal of the Union was merely a means to attain an end, and those who advocated that measure . . . were now willing to try the effect of a reformed House of Commons'.[6] Reform was the point to be gained at that stage and he subordinated Repeal to gain it.

Another subordination of principle to the exigencies of power politics was O'Connell's saving the Whig government from defeat in 1836 by voting to support the Factories Regulation Amendment Bill which

was designed to remove children aged twelve from
[82] the protection of shorter working hours under the
Factories Regulation Act. In 1832 and 1833 O'Connell
had intervened four times in favour of raising the age
and was to do so again in 1839. He supported the
1836 amendment, which was later withdrawn,
because he wished to prevent any prospect of the
return of the Tories to the control of the Irish administration. His opportunistic behaviour, his realism,
damaged his reputation among radicals but his flexi-
bility as to means was essential to his political genius.

4

To estimate O'Connell's politics during the 1830s
some outline of the basic problems in Irish society
after Emancipation is necessary. The central problem
was economic and centred on the land system and the
rising population. Given the limited possibilities for
politicians to change property relations, political
debate tended to focus on the enormous social con-
sequences of Ireland's troubled economy, especially
poverty and lack of education. Ireland's religious
problem – the scandal of vast church wealth and
privileges belonging to a Protestant minority and
supported by a Catholic majority – was part of the
great contemporary debate about church and state.
The political problems included parliamentary and
local government reform and were to be resolved
by disposing of sectarian influence rather than by
advancing the democratic movement.

Fundamental to O'Connell's policy was the hope
of reconciliation, in the interests of Ireland, between
Protestants and Catholics. He never discovered a
political formula which would unite Protestants and
Catholics. Of course his Repeal Party had a significant
number of Protestant MPs: thirteen of the thirty-nine

Repeal MPs in 1832 were Protestants with landed back-
grounds. This was a tribute to Protestant nationalism
of the eighteenth-century variety but O'Connell failed
to establish real unity between Irish Tory Protestantism
and Irish political Catholicism. When he tried in the
1830s his image as a Catholic champion and a radical
determined how Protestants would react.

O'Connell himself accepted that he was only well
acquainted with three provinces of Ireland — Leinster,
Munster and Connaught.[7] In November 1830 Sir
Robert Bateson, the Londonderry MP, reminded
O'Connell that 99 out of 100 people in Ulster would
oppose Repeal and O'Connell accepted that it was
unpopular in the north of Ireland: 'He knew, however, that the people of three provinces had declared
themselves decidedly in its favour'.[8] In the 1834
Repeal debate in the Commons, Spring Rice pointedly
asked the Repealers if they thought that they 'could
compel the sturdy spirits of the North to submit
without a struggle? The struggle would immediately
commence between them; but when it would close,
who is bold enough to say?' To O'Connell this was a
'game of playing us off, one against another'; the MP
for Belfast had seconded Spring Rice in opposing
O'Connell's motion.[9] The Emancipation struggle had
shown that Ulster was diverging very sharply from the
emerging pattern of O'Connellite politics and this was
confirmed in the general election of 1832–3 when
Repeal found little or no support in the fifteen
constituencies of Ulster (76, 51). O'Connell misread
the liberal Presbyterians when he attacked Henry
Montgomery for not supporting Repeal: Montgomery's reply scorned and abused O'Connell but
also, more significantly, stressed the fear of a Dublin
parliament, even in liberal Presbyterian minds, because
O'Connell would be dominant in it and was perceived
as despotic and sectarian.[10] The liberal Presbyterians

had already lost the advantage to Rev. Henry Cooke,
whose dominance and Tory proclivities in Ulster effectively confined O'Connell to the three other provinces. In 1832 O'Connell attempted to have a Tory candidate in Dublin in the Repeal interest but Tory resentment and party spirit was imposssible to overcome. In February 1833, in the midst of his great fight against the Coercion Bill, O'Connell authorised P. V. Fitzpatrick to explore a possible basis of co-operation between Repealers and the Tories led by Dr Boyton, who had asked Fitzpatrick 'whether it was not possible to find a *common ground* on which the two great Irish parties could stand together'. O'Connell attempted to show that English domination affected Irish people of all parties and he outlined his terms: he was prepared to preserve 'all vested interests', to abhor any Catholic supremacy, and to guarantee Protestant equality with Catholics. Boyton was to be told that O'Connell's plan was

> to restore the Irish parliament with the full assent of Protestants and Presbyterians as well as Catholics. I desire no social revolution, no social change. The nobility to possess lands, title and legislative privileges as before the Union. The clergy, *for their lives,* their full incomes — to decrease as Protestantism may allow that decrease. The Landed Gentry to enjoy their present state, being *residents,* . . . In short, salutary restoration without revolution, an Irish parliament, British connection, one King, two legislatures (V, 1957).

This was a bargaining posture and did not reflect his political ideals but it was 'delightful' as a 'vision' of possible reconciliation. O'Connell's terms were very far removed from his own radical beliefs but he was prepared to subordinate his beliefs to political unity between the parties in Ireland, just as he had subordinated his radicalism to the Catholic Emancipation struggle. O'Connell emerges less as the conservative from these negotiations than as the practical politician whose distinguishing characteristic was a lack of dogmatism. Boyton finally rejected O'Connell's proposal because of a 'detestation of Popery'. O'Connell for his part felt compelled to attack the 'vested interests', such as tithes, of the Protestant Establishment in the absence of a Tory-Repeal coalition. In March 1833 he had his proposal put to Sheehan of the *Mail,* another Tory leader, and was in favour of 'giving them every practicable and possible security' asking 'Would *they* take up *the Repeal* as founded on the basis of a local parliament for *local objects* merely and the present 105 members to come over to the Imperial Parliament for all *general* purposes as at present? In short, see what we can do to satisfy him and his' (V, 1967). Tories were unable to respond to O'Connell's flexible overtures because of their ideological commitment to resist the rise of democratic Catholicism. In July 1834 O'Connell again wanted to put to Sheehan 'a treaty for a reconciliation' and composed a document headed 'Basis of an Arrangement to combine persons of all Persuasions in Ireland in Defence of their Common Country, and for the Repeal of Union'. He wished for equality between Catholics and Protestants but with the rights and properties of Protestants secured; for the suppression of both Orange and Ribbon societies and the disestablishment of the Church of Ireland but existing incumbents to retain their vested interests for life. He also proposed that churches be supported voluntarily and that legislation be passed to compel absentees to spend part of their rents in Ireland. He imagined that if the Orange party saw that they could not return to power and dominance and 'if they knew the proper time to make a satisfactory arrangement with their countrymen' they might support Repeal. O'Connell himself, though, was coming to believe 'that it was not possible to conciliate the Orangeists. But I feel it a duty to try' (V, 2087).

By April 1835 Melbourne's government, through his influence, was about to change the personnel and direction of the Irish administration. O'Connell was 'obdurate' that the 'Orange faction' must be cleared out of government. 'How idle to suppose that I can compromise with such a party! I may forgive them, as I ought for myself, but I should be a villain if I did or could forgive for Ireland – that is if I consented to leave them the power to injure Ireland.' O'Connell's 'five years of conciliation' had taught him about the Orange faction 'that it is a faction which may be beaten, but cannot possibly be otherwise conciliated or even mitigated' (V, 2229). O'Connell's principal object was 'to overthrow the Orange system' and to give Catholics equality and fair treatment: this was his principal gain in the Whig Alliance. He gave a 'decisive check to Orangeism' (V, 2235).

O'Connell ignored Ulster sentiment until the 1840s when he declined Cooke's challenge for a face to face debate on Repeal. Cooke told him 'when you *invade* Ulster, and unfurl the flag of Repeal, you will find yourself in a new climate'. Besides religious prejudice Cooke had one unanswerable argument against Repeal: 'Look at Belfast, and be a Repealer if you can: . . . look at the town of Belfast. When I was myself a youth I remember it almost a village. But what a glorious sight does it now present – the masted grove within our harbour – *(cheers)* – our mighty warehouses teeming with the wealth of every climate – *(cheers)* . . . all this we owe to the Union'.[11] In November 1830 O'Connell told Anglesey, the new Lord Lieutenant, that 'the evils of Ireland lie more than skin-deep. There is a morbidity which reaches the heart's core of the social state' (IV, 1732). [87] O'Connell believed that the 'monstrous Church establishment', the drain of absenteeism and the oppressive Protestant monopoly were amongst the chief evils of the Irish social system and to remove them he had to confront Protestant and Tory reaction which, though he hardly realised to what extent, was finding vital new sources of support in the economic development of Ulster under the Union.

5

In the general election of 1832–33 O'Connell made the first independent assault on the Irish representation and the result was a Repeal Party with thirty-nine pledged MPs, the largest single Irish party. O'Connell was disappointed with the Irish Reform Act as it did not enlarge the Irish franchise sufficiently or give Ireland the twenty-five extra seats he had sought with good reason on a population basis. Clearly the Whigs wished to prevent a revolutionary transfer of power in Ireland and O'Connell was prevented from controlling the entire Irish representation. To build his new party O'Connell had to overcome major difficulties, including the property qualification for MPs, the limited franchise, the cost of supporting MPs in London at their own or the party's expense and the great expense of elections and petitions against election results. His Repeal Party was necessarily 'overwhelmingly landed' in character with very strong family connections: eight MPs were related or connected to O'Connell (76, 76–7). O'Connell built up a working central organisation with paid party agents and he co-ordinated at least twenty-four local county clubs in terms of the registration of voters, selection of candidates and policy changes. He acted as a party leader, regularly touring constituencies, 'nursing' influential people or organisations and influencing and supporting the press. He also led the MPs in the House of Commons where party discipline had hitherto been informal.

O'Connell's parliamentary tactics in 1832–34 taught the Whigs the value of his co-operation and the difficulties of his opposition. The classic parliamentary exhibition by O'Connell occurred during the 1833 session when he engaged in a prolonged battle over the severe Coercion Bill brought forward to curb the tithe agitation but which, if passed before O'Connell 'plucked the fangs out of it' in Sheil's phrase, would have prevented political organisation. O'Connell's opposition began with the King's Speech which he described as 'a bloody, and brutal address' and he contended that crime in Ireland was the result of misgovernment, not agitation. O'Connell's speeches against the Coercion Bill indicted the government and spelled out Irish grievances; as Lecky declared they should be read by all 'who desire to understand O'Connell and his times' (35, 135). O'Connell prophesied that if the Whigs suppressed Irish politics 'there would be, not a moral revolution or a political revolution but a revolution of the sword in Ireland'.[12] With his small band of MPs he fought the bill at every stage and by all possible means, dividing at every opportunity, prolonging debates, initiating general discussions on Irish affairs, analysing in committee, and appealing for support outside parliament. Attacking the Whigs for having 'brains of lead, hearts of stone, and fangs of iron', O'Connell put on a sustained and impressive parliamentary performance which compares, as MacDonagh points out, with Parnell's strategy and *modus operandi* in the 1880s as an exercise in parliamentary skills (72, 50). O'Connell openly proposed obstructive tactics and only Stanley, his opponent, declaring that Repeal should be 'resisted to the death' rose to match O'Connell's effort. O'Neill Daunt believed that the 1833 session was 'the crowning glory' of O'Connell's parliamentary career (*20,* I, 9). O'Connell succeeded in 'emasculating' the bill 'far beyond my hopes' and he told Fitzpatrick that as passed it was 'more a foolish than an infernal bill' (V, 1966).

The Repeal Party, through the influence of Feargus O'Connor, divided on the question of when to bring forward Repeal in the Commons. O'Connell managed to defer it for as long as possible but in April 1834 he was forced to introduce a Repeal motion: 'I felt', he told O'Neill Daunt, 'like a man who was going to jump into a cold bath, but I was obliged to take the plunge' (*20,* I, 18). O'Connell's speech outlined the case for Repeal to an unwilling House and did not influence any British MPs to take up the cause. The main effect, in fact, was to remove Repeal from practical parliamentary politics, and thus pave the way for the Lichfield House Compact between the Whigs and O'Connell in 1835.

O'Connell fought the 1835 general election, which resulted in the Whigs losing their overall majority, on a 'No Tories, No Tithes' slogan under an Anti-Tory Association. It was, in effect, a Whig-Repeal coalition. The Tories might attack the Whig 'partnership with rebellion' but O'Connell had secured vital leverage over the Melbourne government, as his MPs were now essential to its survival in office. Thus it was that personal attacks on O'Connell became the most convenient method of discrediting the Whigs — became, indeed, an accepted convention of political life. Right through the 1830s there were episodes which severely damaged O'Connell in terms of public opinion in Britain — his abusive language calling Hardinge a 'paltry, contemptible little English soldier',

calling Alvaney a 'bloated buffoon', becoming em-
broiled with Disraeli in an exchange which did neither
much credit, the Raphael incident when O'Connell
was accused of selling a seat in parliament, the Ellen
Courtenay propaganda against him on the grounds
of immorality, O'Connell's attacks on the perjury
of Tory election committees in the House and his
propensity to refer to 'Saxons' — all these and more
created a very unfavourable 'persona' for O'Connell in
Britain. O'Connell was a 'ruffian', a 'public swindler',
and wholly disreputable in Tory eyes.

The Whig programme of Irish reforms became a
key battleground for the Tories; for some of them it
was a rearguard action. O'Connell's compact with the
Whigs emerged from meetings at Lichfield House, the
Earl of Lichfield's residence, in March and April 1835
attended by O'Connellite and Whig MPs. There was
no written agreement but there was a clear understanding based upon an exchange of political advantages. O'Connell obtained a liberal Irish administration
and Whig undertakings to reform the Protestant
Church establishment, extend the Reform Act to
Ireland on the same basis as in England and to reform
local government. The Whigs got office. Of course,
the extent of their Irish reforms would depend upon
their ability to get their measures through the Tory
House of Lords. In February 1835 O'Connell intended
to give the Whigs a 'trial to show whether *they* could
produce good government in Ireland, and if that
experiment failed, I would come back with tenfold
force to the Repeal' (V, 2216).

6

O'Connell's alliance with the Melbourne ministry
between 1835 and 1841 was a success because of
the conduct and the character of the Irish administra-

tion during the period. The legislative results, while important, had as many frustrations as satisfactions for O'Connell and from 1838 he was preparing to reactivate mass agitation. He gained a settlement of the tithe question though he lost the appropriation clause which would have applied Church funds for social purposes; he finally gained an emasculated Municipal Corporations Act in 1840 which, while unsatisfactory, gave him the opportunity to become Lord Mayor of Dublin and with it Catholics took a major step forward in local government; the Poor Law Commission of 1836 was ignored and the unfortunate and ill-considered replacement, the Poor Law Act of 1838, greatly dissatisfied O'Connell but at least Catholics in the Poor Law Boards of Guardian elections made further inroads on local governing bodies.

It was Lord Mulgrave as Lord Lieutenant, Lord Morpeth, the Chief Secretary and Thomas Drummond, the Under-Secretary, who made O'Connell's parliamentary frustrations worthwhile. These three men, unequivocally liberal and popular in their politics, were deeply committed to the improvement of Ireland. Drummond, in particular, worked like a slave and died in 1840 when his health eventually proved unable to bear the weight of work. Under these men, the Irish administration governed in the interests of the whole population. The relationship between O'Connell and the Castle was close and cordial, to the dismay of the 'Orangeists' and Tories. Emancipation became for the first time something of a reality with the appointments made by the new administration. The law officers were all 'liberal' and four of them were Catholics. A policy of promotions from 'among the friends of the people' was openly enunciated. It was a triumph O'Connell savoured, bearing in mind his long exclusion and victimisation, especially

as those now appointed had integrity and a high
degree of competence.

The government sought to counteract the political bias of the existing judges and to appoint sheriffs and magistrates acceptable to the Catholic population. They did not shrink from dismissing magistrates for misdemeanours. Colonel Verner was sacked in 1837 for publicly toasting the Protestant victory over Catholics at the 'Battle of the Diamond'. Clear instructions were issued to the army, police, and magistrates and public rebukes to magistrates such as Drummond's famous reply to the magistrates of Tipperary that 'property has its duties as well as its rights' in 1838. Drummond employed a greater number of stipendiary (professional) magistrates which encouraged an even-handed system of justice; he also improved the operation of the petty session courts. Across the range of the administration there was an 'intense vigilance and bureaucratic zeal at central government level, and a Fabianesque permeation of existing structures and institutions', seeking to liberalise and render the state acceptable to the population (97, 15). A positive result was the considerable diminution of popular violence throughout Irish society: for the first time since the Union a government went through its six-year term of office without having to seek 'exceptional' legislation to pacify Ireland.

O'Connell saw the liberal administration in Ireland as more important than the actual measures passed by the Whigs. After eight years of agitation the Tithe Act of 1838 ended the 'tithe war' in a compromise. There had been a very large element of spontaneity in the agitation which had seemed to contemporaries to threaten 'a wholesale war against property'. O'Connell's contribution was to give the agitation political direction and to attempt to impose nonviolent techniques on the anti-tithe movement. He declared he would never pay tithes and he made it an election issue right through the 1830s. At local level the nexus between the anti-tithe popular struggle and the O'Connellite political organisation was complete. Tithe agitation was an important factor in the Repeal success in 1832–33 (*76*, 53). O'Connell himself used this powerful issue with great emotional effect as when he had 'the people in tears upon the topic of the Rathcormac murders' in 1835 during the Kerry election (V, 2184). His parliamentary struggle succeeded in having arrears of tithes between 1834 and 1837 written off. The Act operated at the expense of Irish landlordism in the long run, as tenant resistance had only one focus left when tithes became a rent charge: the landlord.

Irish Church Reform had begun in a limited way with the Irish Church Temporalities Act. After this, in Lecky's phrase, 'it continued to be an anomaly' but 'it ceased to be a scandal'. The measure introduced in 1833 abolished church cess raised from Catholics and Protestants and replaced it by a tax on clerical incomes. Ten of the twenty-two bishoprics were removed from the Church Establishment. The proposal in the bill to create a fund by allowing the tenants on the bishops' extensive estates to buy their land outright in place of short-term leases and to use this fund to pay the bishops the equivalent of their former rents while leaving the surplus at parliament's disposal had to be dropped, much to O'Connell's fury. For the 1830s it was quite a sweeping reform of the Irish Protestant Church but it was not politically possible to devote or 'appropriate' the surplus from the sale of episcopal lands to parliamentary expenditure 'for religious and charitable purposes'. O'Connell was disappointed that this first step on the road to disestablishment was not taken and he continued to

seek full disestablishment. He never succeeded in
[94] making this a significant parliamentary question
during the period of the Lichfield House Alliance
but the question of 'appropriating' church funds to
parliamentary purposes bedevilled Whig attempts to
solve the tithe question between 1835 and 1837. Due
to the hostility this aroused the Tithe Act of 1838
contained no 'appropriation' clause.

The final great measure which resulted from the
Whig alliance was municipal reform which passed
through parliament in 1840. O'Connell saw the
potential of local government for nationalist agitation
as his endlessly quoted remark of 1836 confirms:
O'Connell declared he saw in each corporate town
'a Normal school for teaching the science of peaceful
political agitation'.[13] The Irish measure of municipal
reform may have been 'a most limited and conservative measure' as compared with Scottish and English
reform (76, 227) but compared with what existed
before 1840 it was a radical change. O'Connell had
long recognised that ending the Protestant monopoly
of corporate rights and their control of the administration of justice which followed upon their monopoly
was 'the hinge on which the reformation of corporations turns' (V, 1969). After O'Connell's Whig alliance
Irish local government, while confused, allowed for
popular participation by O'Connellite forces. Ten
towns had elected councils in the Repeal interest;
Boards of Guardians were elected and influenced by
O'Connellite organisations at local level; O'Connellite
MPs had influence in the selection of sheriffs who
selected grand juries in the counties and many towns
had popularly elected Boards of Commissions under
the 1828 Act. Representative bodies were growing up
which were to have a profound influence upon the
future course of nationalist agitation in Ireland.

7

O'Connell's attitude to the Poor Law requires closer [95] analysis because it helps to throw light on his social and economic views. Irish poverty was so great that it inevitably led to a discussion of the whole Irish social and economic position, in particular the role of the state in economic life. The general 'establishment' attitude towards the Irish economy stemmed from a synthesis of Malthus' population thesis, Ricardo's capitalist theories and Bentham's view of a spontaneous economic system in which interests must be allowed to find their own natural harmony with a minimum of outside or government interference (76, 203). To what extent did O'Connell share this attitude? Very early in his House of Commons career he spoke on distress in Ireland and argued that it was the duty of parliament to afford relief or at least inquire into Irish distress.[14] O'Connell's economic stance was always coloured by his opposition to 'odious oligarchy', to the aristocrats, in effect. In November 1830 he introduced a motion for the repeal of the Sub-Letting Act because it was making it easier for landlords to clear their estates. Of course, the supporters of the Act accepted this, arguing that it was necessary to clear Irish estates and to establish in Ireland a capitalist agriculture. But to O'Connell

> This was the argument of heartless and unfeeling men, who thought it better to support upon an estate a great many beasts and very few human beings, than a large population . . . it was not, he contended, the part of a considerate and humane Government to make itself the auxiliary of the landlord. . . . From the period of the Union until the present, all the Statutes enacted by the Legislature had had for their object the oppression of the peasantry, and the giving of advantage to the landlord.

O'Connell denied the benefits of capitalist farming, rejecting pages of evidence 'which unfeeling men had given in favour of cultivating sheep and cattle instead of human beings': the Sub-Letting Act was 'a political economy measure not a Government Act'. O'Connell might see the benefits of large farms but he argued that the Act had not created them and that the super-abundance of labour in Ireland was due to bad laws and bad government.[15] Thus his fundamental position was for a definite role for the state in economic life; indeed his whole Repeal agitation rested on the belief that Irish economic problems derived from the absence of an Irish parliament to deal with them. O'Connell supported state grants for public works, a tax on absentee landlords, security for tenants as opposed to landlords and an end to the oppression suffered by the people in the administration of justice. He was always anxious to stimulate inter-ference by the state to relieve distress in Ireland (VI, 2629) and he supported state grants to develop Irish railways (VI, 2630).

O'Connell, then, did not share the general laissez-faire analysis of Irish problems. He was opposed to a Poor Law for Ireland on the basis of English experi-ence. He believed that poorhouses would bring moral degradation on the inmates and simply change 'the mode of suffering' for the poor (V, 2324). He opposed employment for the able-bodied out of poor rates because poor rates did not increase capital investment in Ireland but 'only distributes it in a different and less economic and less sagacious mode'. Ireland's tenant farmers could not afford poor rates and O'Connell objected to supporters of the bill being 'benevolent and humane at the expense of others' (V, 2325). To O'Connellites, such as Father Sheehan, and to O'Connell himself, the Poor Law Bill was 'emphatically a landlord's bill' which would stimulate evictions and increase pauperism and leave the absentees untouched (VI, 2482). O'Connell nick- named it the Irish 'Destitution' Bill: never, he believed 'was cant more conspicuous than in the cry of some of our Poor Law mongers' — a Poor Law 'affords less relief than it inflicts injury' and O'Connell opposed it in the Commons (VI, 2502). He failed to defeat or amend it partly because Irish opinion tended to be favourable, influenced especially by Bishop Doyle. O'Connell believed that the ratepayers, especially 'the occupiers', would have to carry an additional tax of one million and all this for 'imprisonment in a work-house' (VI, 2505). He recognised however that the poor rate would give him 'a powerful lever' in future campaigns when he was considering his course of action near the end of the Whig alliance (VI, 2658).

O'Connell's alternative to the Poor Law may be deduced from his general political programme. He believed that the Poor Law would dry up private charity and 'destroy the sense of personal independence which still remained in the country'. But he did not contemplate mere acceptance of the *status quo*. He supported the Commission of Inquiry which sat between 1833 and 1836; this eventually recommended a complete series of measures including subsidised emigration, land improvement, agricultural education and a programme of public works. This major report was ignored by the government but when in the 1840s O'Connell began to use the anti-poor rate agitation to build his Repeal campaign the Repeal Association issued a report which favoured fixity of tenure for Irish tenants, the transfer of the burden of poor rates to property owners, a public works programme and the revival of Irish manufactures as alternatives to the Poor Law as operated, though Repeal opinion was divided on the question of total repeal or modification of the Poor Law (*71*, 35—8).

O'Connell's economic measures, while always sub-
[98] ordinated to political aims, were based upon his social
concern, humanitarianism and knowledge of the Irish
situation rather than laissez-faire dogma. He hoped to
keep (indeed political conditions forced him to rely
upon) the landed gentry as the basis of his political
party but he had, as Lecky remarks, 'a good deal of
the feudal feeling of his class' and he cared deeply,
if not altogether wisely, for his own tenantry (35,
179—80). His social concern for his tenants emerges
clearly in his letters to his agent John Primrose as, for
example, during the cholera outbreak in 1834 when
he urged him to 'be prodigal of relief out of my
means' (V, 2047, 2048). It is also clear in his evidence
to the Devon Commission in 1845. It must be remembered, also, that O'Connell was a small landlord with
a relatively tiny annual income from land. In the
latter part of his career he urged the necessity for
new agrarian legislation which would give more
security to tenants and give them compensation for
improvements.

O'Connell has often been charged with being 'anti-
labour', particularly since James Connolly wrote
'A Chapter of Horrors: Daniel O'Connell and the
Working Class' in his *Labour in Irish History* published
in 1910. Connolly argued that secret societies were
'the most effective weapons of the peasantry' in
the 'Tithe War' and that to them the victory largely
belonged; he also declared that politicians gave
'neither help nor countenance to the fight' and that
the Catholic clergy, for selfish reasons, refrained from
condemning secret conspiracy during the agitation
from which they might expect to benefit. Connolly
was wrong in these three respects: it was the sophisticated techniques learned from O'Connell's repertoire
and implemented by his local organisations that
secured success and secret societies were roundly

condemned by the Church, notably Bishop Doyle. Connolly went on to maintain that the Irish working class believed that the decay of Irish trade was due to the Act of Union simply because they accepted 'O'Connell's explanation'. However, Irish workers, and other social groups, were deeply imbued with a political outlook which considered the Act of Union responsible for economic problems. As O'Neill Daunt wrote: 'It is a great mistake to suppose that he [O'Connell] originated the national desire for Repeal'; O'Connell had to reflect it and often had difficulty in putting a brake on Repeal sentiment (*20*, I, 4; *20*, II, 136—7). Repeal was for organised artisans a socio-economic objective which would restore economic prosperity and they did not simply follow O'Connell, as Connolly maintained, because they believed him to be insincere in his loyalty or in his profession of limited aims. There is an entire absence of any serious social critique within the organised labour movement in Ireland during the period. Connolly concluded by declaring that O'Connell ceased after 1835 'to play for the favour of organised labour', that he gradually developed into 'the most bitter and unscrupulous enemy of trade unionism Ireland has yet produced', and that he attacked the trades unions in Dublin by throwing 'all his force on the side of capitalist privilege and against social reform'.

In fact O'Connell was the 'friend and advocate' of working men, who could speak in terms of 'a master class and a slave class' and who was a member of the London Working Men's Association. He regarded the 'working classes' as being 'borne down' by the 'double effects of increasing machinery' and 'undiminished taxation' and he believed that all should have the franchise exercised through secret ballot in order to remedy oppression (VI, 2485a). He opposed violent activities through secret combination in

Dublin between 1836 and 1838 but supported peaceful and legal activities by trades unions. In the Commons in 1838 he defended the freedom of workers to combine for the purpose of raising wages or to prevent them being lowered; the employers, he argued, also committed 'crimes' of combination but as they were protected by their wealth it was impossible to detect them 'but the poor man was easily detected and punished'.[16] He praised labour leaders in Dublin and wished to include employers in the parliamentary inquiry. However, he did oppose the monopoly of certain workers which was imposed by violence and coercion. He also argued for the need to create a demand for labour in Ireland by attracting investment from capitalists who ought to be offered security; this would bring a gradual and progressive improvement in the conditions of labouring men. He recognised that the Dublin unions of the time were exclusively unions of skilled workers and thus were more privileged than the general labouring population; he opposed enforced membership of unions and restrictive activities such as limitations on apprentices. He believed that combinations, of a secret and violent kind, affected wages and employment and damaged the interests of workers even more than employers (VI, 2485a). He was prepared to meet the artisans in open debate at a time of unprecedented labour unrest and violence, despite the physical dangers to himself. This was not a classic encounter of the labour and capitalist viewpoints (52, 238) but a confrontation on the techniques for labour agitation. O'Connell succeeded in persuading the artisans to use moral pressure and public opinion, not 'the bludgeon and the knobstick'.

During the 1840s O'Connell had the support of the trades unions who eschewed labour violence and there was no further strain or collision in the relationship. He proceeded from libertarian arguments to defend 'individual liberty' and some of his economic ideas about wages and capital were simply the current coin of the day; neither the artisans nor O'Connell were in favour of a social or economic revolution as a remedy for Irish problems. However, O'Connell's social concern, together with his defence of the Tolpuddle Martyrs and the right of artisans to meet and organise, as well as his guidance on agitation techniques makes him a most significant figure in Irish labour history.

8

In the later 1830s O'Connell was the victim of his own success. Good government in Ireland was not conducive to the popular agitation upon which his political career depended financially but also, in a much deeper way, psychologically. 'The aching void left craving at my heart' was his own description of the effect of his wife's death in 1836 (VI, 2456). After her death O'Connell lost some of his sureness of touch in his political career. Mary had always reassured him, as no one else could, as when she wrote to him in December 1830 following his rejection of Whig offers which would have drawn his teeth in any future agitation: 'Had you been betrayed into the acceptance of the terms offered by Government you would die of a broken heart before six months expired' (IV, 1737). Now his policy of being 'wedded to Ireland' in the late 1830s had brought him to a low point in popularity; he was in his sixties and was turning to religion for personal consolation (VI, 2369a). His policy of getting 'something for Ireland' was hardly a soul-stirring one, whatever about its real practical merit. Having London as the centre of political activity and the subtle corrosive effects of the Whig alliance had dissolved his political party. Any small party is in danger when allied to a larger. Future nationalist parties in Ireland were to be ruined through the pressures of a Liberal alliance.

O'Connell had no special answer to this political consequence of the Union. He thought about Repeal as his first effort in politics and toyed with the idea of it being his last, though to hope for success seemed 'idle' (VI, 2542). The Whigs were clearly on the way out even if they managed a few more years in office; other Irish MPs had obtained office and in June 1838 O'Connell was offered the position of Master of the Rolls in Ireland which would have allowed him to end his political career in dignity. With a heavy heart he made the sacrifice and refused (VI, 2546). In August he launched the Precursor Society to fight one more parliamentary session for justice in Ireland. If that failed a Repeal agitation was to be mounted. O'Connell would not desert the Whigs since the alternative was the Tories; this despite the fact that 'their incompetency to do us good' almost equalled 'their unwillingness to exert themselves for us' (VI, 2560). By August 1839 this drifting policy had nearly ruined his career, as he told his confidant Fitzpatrick. His unhappiness stemmed from 'the desertion of me by the country at large', a blow to his self-identification with Ireland which he knew himself he could not survive (VI, 2645).

> My own prospects appear to me to be daily darker and more dark. It does mortify me but it does not surprise me to find I have exhausted the bounty of the Irish people. God help me! What shall I do? . . . I want a period of retreat to think of nothing but eternity. I sigh when I look at the present agitated aspect of affairs, foreign and domestic, and vainly think that if Ireland thought fit to support me I might still be useful; but it is plain I have worn out

my claim on the people ... I am, I believe, on the verge of illness — the illness of despondency but it is clear I have no one to blame but myself. . . . Still I do not regret that I gave up my profession and refused office (VI, 2646). [103]

Next day he writes of his dislike at 'the idea of terminating my political career and shrinking into obscurity' but this seemed inevitable (VI, 2648). Yet by the end of that month he was developing a new plan of agitation which was first to take him to fresh heights of grandeur before plunging him into despair and final decline (VI, 2657, 2658).

5
'A Prophet of a Coming Time'

Besides being a great and a good man he was also a disappointed man. The sight of his promised land was not given to his longing eyes. But as a prophet of a coming time he fulfilled his mission. (*59*, 168)

1

Paradoxically, O'Connell's international reputation was rising to a new peak just as his career seemed finished in Ireland in the late 1830s. O'Connell's Ireland took its place with Napoleonic France or Jacksonian America as one of the great contemporary phenomena in world affairs:

Go where you will on the Continent: visit any coffee house; dine at any public table; embark on board of any steamboat; enter any diligence, any railway carriage; from the moment that your accent shows you to be an Englishman, the very first question asked by your companions, be they what they may, physicians, advocates, merchants, manufacturers, or what we should call yeomen, is certain to be 'What will be done with Mr O'Connell?' Look over any file of French journals; and you will see what a space he occupies in the eyes of the French people.

When Macaulay reported thus to the House of Commons in February 1844 he was, without exaggeration, acknowledging O'Connell's achievement in securing for Ireland more international attention than she had ever achieved in modern history. O'Connell's popular democracy caught European attention in an exceptional way during the second quarter of the nineteenth century. Gustave de Beaumont came to Ireland with his life-long friend and political associate, Alexis de Tocqueville, in the 1830s to do for Ireland what Tocqueville had accomplished in his masterpiece *Democracy in America,* the first part of which was published in 1835. This work was, as John Stuart Mill observed, the start of 'a new era in the scientific study of politics' and given Tocqueville's and Beaumont's absorbing interest in the rise of democracy it was revealing when they turned from the United States, 'the image of democracy itself', to Ireland, where O'Connell had created the first liberal Catholic and democratic movement. Beaumont's work *Ireland, Social, Political and Religious* was published in 1839 and proved the most popular of nineteenth-century continental books in Ireland. Beaumont's analysis of O'Connell and his organisation in the context of Irish conditions was masterly. He saw O'Connell as a product of Irish history and circumstances:

> The great men who seem to conduct the age very often give it expression; it is believed that they lead the world, they only comprehend it; they have perceived the necessities of which they constitute themselves the defenders and divined the passions of which they make themselves the organs. (*7,* II, 73)

O'Connell himself, according to his early biographer, Fagan, used to say that he was 'like a straw floating on the surface of a deep stream which showed how the current ran' (*29,* II, 206). Beaumont explained to a European audience the significance of O'Connell's leadership in Ireland in terms of the rise of democratic

politics. For other Europeans O'Connell's liberal
Catholicism was even more significant.

O'Connell was the first European politician to
achieve significant victories for the cause of civil and
religious liberty in the oppressive age of Metternich
by applying 'moral force', that is, disciplined public
opinion. What made him unique was that he combined his advanced liberal achievements with his
Catholicism. He espoused the principle of the separation of church and state. History had made the Irish
Catholic Church a 'poor' church, dependent upon the
voluntary commitment of its members and independent of the state apparatus. It provided a working
model of O'Connell's ideal relationship (IV, 1669).
He was an opponent both of the Protestant Church
as a state supported establishment and of any state
control over the Catholic Church (IV, 1709). O'Connell changed the way Catholics saw the relationship
between the church and society in post-Revolution-
ary Europe. His contribution to liberal Catholic movements in European countries from the 1820s onward
was enormous. In 1815 in the Veto controversy, he
had argued the limited power of the Pope in spiritual
matters (he subjected it to the national hierarchy of
Catholic bishops) and he declared that the Pope had
no temporal powers (3, II, 178).

To express principles of civil and religious liberty
was vital but what was unique was that O'Connell put
them into practice. Rome came to realise that Irish
Catholicism was something separate from British
Catholicism and that it was the specific concern of
the Irish Catholic Church. This combination of full
civil and religious liberty with fidelity to the Catholic
religion fascinated European liberal Catholics. Further,
O'Connell envisaged the social role of the Catholic
Church, from Gospel precepts, as being on the side of
the poor and oppressed. Thus he wished to array

Catholicity behind the abolition of the Corn Laws which allowed 'the plunder of the poor for the bene- fit of the rich'; the role of the Catholic Church was to be 'at the side of the people; the mitigator of poverty and the comforter of the distressed; the opponent of aristocratic selfishness; the true guardian of the poor of the Lord' (*14*, 8).

O'Connell had to work hard to win over the Irish Catholic bishops as a *national* hierarchy. He conceived a special destiny for Ireland, 'that of Catholicising other nations' (*20*, II, 293) and he bound up Catholic religious and ecclesiastical ambitions with self-government for the Irish people. It is clear that the revival of the Repeal agitation in the 1840s required O'Connell to spell out a special relationship with the Catholic Church in order to secure its support in the campaign. He did this to Paul Cullen, Rector of the Irish College in Rome, who was destined to fulfil O'Connell's ambition when he became an Irish cardinal (VII, 2959). O'Connell showed the advantages that 'Catholicity' would derive from Repeal, even to the extent that Protestantism 'would not survive ten years' as Irish Protestants were 'political protestants, that is, Protestants by reason of their participation in political power' to the exclusion of Catholics. Catholic dioceses would receive greater voluntary support and obtain the necessary property when Catholics were relieved of the tithe-rent charge. He held forth a glowing future for the Catholic Church under Repeal which went dangerously close to compromising the secularity of the state to be established by Repeal. He had already signalled to Archbishop MacHale in 1839 that in a Dublin parliament there would be Catholic control over education for Catholics (VI, 2670). By clearly seeking a rally of 'Catholic Ireland' and conceding vital domains to the Catholic Church, O'Connell succeeded in obtaining

MacHale's powerful support for the Repeal agitation
in 1840. He clearly committed himself in July 1840
in a private communication to MacHale:

> In short, if we had the Repeal,
> Religion would be free
> Education would be free
> The press would be free
> No sectarian control over Catholics; no Catholic
> control over sectarians; that is, no species of
> political ascendancy. The law would of course
> sanction in the fullest measure the spiritual author-
> ity of the episcopal order over religious discipline
> amongst Catholics including Catholic education
> (VI, 2730).

This compact between Irish nationalist movements
and the Catholic Church was to be the basis of all
future constitutional movements for legislative independence in Ireland. For O'Connell it sowed the seeds
of the later dispute in 1844—45 which helped to
alienate the small band of Protestant supporters led
by Davis in the Repeal Association.

2

O'Connell had a sense of his European and world
significance. He had faith in his new political techniques and the particular role the Irish Catholic people
were to play abroad. 'The moral force doctrine *will*
prevail', he told O'Neill Daunt, 'other nations will
learn from us. They are watching us now with astonish-
ment'. He believed that physical violence would become 'quite obsolete' (*20,* II, 178—9). He took a deep
interest in Australian and Canadian affairs and supported the development of 'free institutions' and the
self-government of the colonies. He championed the
blacks in the West Indies, and held that no distinction

should be made between free settlers and emancipated convicts in Australia. His Irish political organisations contributed to the political effectiveness of Irish emigrants, notably in the United States. O'Connell received important support for his movements from the Irish abroad but as an abolitionist and advocate of full civil rights for blacks he alienated his Irish-American support. To O'Connell human slavery was 'an outrage of natural right and natural law, which no lapse of time, and no combination of circumstances' could make 'a rightful and a just state of things' (*16*, I, 44).

After his participation in the successful struggle for the abolition of slavery in the British Empire O'Connell was chiefly responsible for directing the force of the British anti-slavery movement into the camp of the American abolitionists. He was of crucial importance to moral force abolitionism and he was portrayed in 'heroic dimensions' in America as 'the exemplary international humanitarian of the age, a man whose literal belief in the brotherhood of man forbade him to take a compliant stand on American slavery for the sake of financial support for his domestic political goals from the overseas Irish (*95*, 899). O'Connell was a bitter critic of Americans who favoured slavery and yet claimed to be supporters of the ideals of the American Revolution. His conception of himself as 'a universal reformer' in support of 'humankind', as he had imagined his role in his student days of the 1790s, had not disappeared. Rather it had deepened: 'I want no American aid, if it comes across the Atlantic stained in negro blood', he declared in May 1845. His stance was unpopular with Young Irelanders such as John Mitchel who acquiesced in racialism; it was even more unpopular amongst Irish-Americans and, in effect, O'Connell sacrificed the Irish-American wing of his movement to the cause of

abolition of slavery and disrupted Irish-American
[110] influence in the United States for a generation.

O'Connell's internationalism and concern for the
oppressed throughout the world was an integral part
of his life and career. His powerful Cincinnati letter
of 1843, in reply to the Cincinnati Repeal Association, is one of the great documents of his life:

> We next refer to your declaration that the two
> races, viz., the black and the white, cannot exist on
> equal terms under your government and your in-
> stitutions. This is an extraordinary assertion to be
> made at the present day. You allude indeed to
> Antigua and the Bermudas; but we will take you to
> where the experiment has been successfully made
> upon a large scale, namely, to Jamaica. There the
> two races are upon a perfect equality in point of
> law — there is no master, there is no slave; the law
> does not recognise the slightest distinction between
> the races. You have borrowed the far greater part
> of your address from the cant phraseology which
> the West Indies slave-owners and especially those
> of Jamaica made use of before emancipation . . . In
> short, your prophecies of the destructive effects of
> emancipation are but faint and foolish echoes of
> the prophetic apprehension of the British slave-
> owners. [1]

American, colonial and European views of O'Connell throw the British image of him into relief.
Through Carlyle's influence on Young Ireland, this
British image has had a powerful and damaging effect
upon Irish attitudes.

3

Repeal of the Union was not a simple matter. To give
Ireland her own parliament, with O'Connell as Prime

Minister, would have amounted to a revolution in Irish society and in Anglo-Irish relations. O'Connell envisaged an independent Irish parliament, under the Crown, separate from Westminster. At various times he was prepared to accept less for political reasons but his real objective was Irish legislative independence. He possibly reconciled his alternating pursuits of 'Justice or Repeal' through his belief that justice to Ireland would require eventual restoration of the Irish parliament. Ireland would continue to play a vital part in the British Empire which would progressively give colonies independent legislatures, making the Irish abroad free citizens also. In the summer of 1842, for example, O'Connell fought for Newfoundland's constitution in the Commons (VII, 2962). An Irish parliament would be reformed, quite unlike Grattan's Parliament. O'Connell was an advanced democrat and his Repeal programme called for universal suffrage and the ballot. There would be a House of Lords in which Protestants would predominate but O'Connell would have the Catholic bishops sitting with the Protestant bishops. However, his anti-House of Lords campaign in Britain in the 1830s had not given much confidence to those Protestants who were supposed to see the Lords as a counterweight to the democratic and Catholic Commons.

O'Connell intended to procure justice for Catholics but he would not persecute Protestants or set up any sort of ascendancy; to Protestants, however, Catholic numerical advantages seemed to pre-ordain a Catholic ascendancy. O'Connell sought to build a liberal Irish state with a free Catholic Church under a constitutional monarch. He conceded to all churches the right to control the education of their members and he went close to committing himself to sanction by law 'the spiritual authority of the episcopal order over religious discipline amongst Catholics' (VI, 2730). He would have guaranteed also to other denominations

'perfect religious freedom' and 'freedom of conscience'.

O'Connell saw politics as an instrument of 'improvement': his democratic politics depended upon compromise, the willingness to accept less than the original demand, the notion that some 'improvement' was better than no progress at all. Isaac Butt claimed that 'Repeal was a revolution' in his great debate with O'Connell in 1843. O'Connell would have dismantled the Protestant Church Establishment and would have facilitated a social revolution through the status gained by Catholics in an Irish parliament. The grip of the Protestant minority on patronage and privilege would have been broken.

What was even more threatening to Protestants was O'Connell's land policy. Sir James Graham's outburst in the House of Commons in June 1843 is revealing: '... unless the House is prepared to adopt the principle of fixity of tenure or agree . . . that the Protestant establishment must be overthrown . . . I do not see what measures of further conciliation can be proposed.' Along with his alliance with the Catholic Church, the second great foundation for the Repeal Association was O'Connell's land policy. In 1841 he pointed out to Bishop Higgins that his 'tenancy plan' would 'secure Ireland for the Irish'; he argued that it would take an enormous movement from the Repeal Association to get the Houses of Parliament even to consider land reform and it obviously increased 'the strength and rapidity of that movement to have this palpable advantage to the Irish farmers as part and parcel of the Repeal' (VII, 2830). He chaired a committee of the Repeal Association in 1841 which recommended tenure of not less than twenty years, compensation for improvements and rents to be fixed by arbitration.

O'Connell supported the Irish Waste Land Improvement Society, founded in 1838 by the Earl of Devon, whose purpose was to buy up tracts of waste land and lease it in small portions to tenants who would be assisted to reclaim it (*49*, 181). O'Connell wished to end the increasing rural destitution and agrarian violence by giving the tenant security and ending 'the enormous power' held by the landlord. He publicly attacked the Devon Commission because only landlords were represented on it as 'a board of foxes deliberating gravely over a flock of geese'. He argued before the Devon Commission that if his solutions seemed 'violent', as they must to men dominated by laissez-faire, they were 'applicable to a violent disease': he would insist upon long leases and would have no rent recoverable except upon leases which he would make cheaper and easier to obtain; he would have rents fixed by 'a compelled arbitration' and the tenant would be free to sell his interest in his holding and to obtain compensation for improvements if he had to give up the holding. He would have taxed the absentee landlords very heavily and would have taken away the power of distraining.[2]

O'Connell was as radical on the land question as it was practicable to be within the confines of a broad national movement hoping to persuade a hostile parliament to make changes. He rejected the agrarian radicalism of William Connor, who proposed that the Repeal movement should adopt a no-rent campaign of passive resistance. He believed that Connor was an enemy of the right of security of property and had him expelled from the Repeal Association (*71*, 177–80). O'Connell was prepared to support measures 'unpalatable' to landlords and to rectify the imbalance in law which they had over tenants but he was not prepared to commence a war against them as a class. For O'Connell 'tenant-right' amounted to the three Fs – fixity of tenure, fair rents, free sale – and com-

pensation for improvements. It was to take another
[114] generation before such measures found any acceptance in Westminster but these proposals go far to
explain popular enthusiasm for Repeal.

Another key Repeal promise was to provide legislative 'encouragement and protection' to Irish manufacturers. O'Connell's Repeal Board of Trade denied
that an independent Irish parliament would construct
a tariff wall against British goods but it was evident
that Irish duties would be imposed on certain goods
and O'Connell was able to attach the Irish manufacture movement to the Repeal campaign. The strength
of the Repeal Movement in the towns depended upon
the perception of Repeal as a socio-economic objective.

The Repeal campaign differed from the Catholic
Emancipation campaign because by the 1840s Catholics
had wrested control of urban local government from
Protestants: the first elections under the Municipal
Corporations Act took place in October 1841. In
Cork Catholics took control of seven of the eight
wards and fifty-six Liberals were elected as against six
Tories. In Dublin, after great expense and effort, the
Liberals won thirteen wards out of fifteen and O'Connell was elected the first Catholic Lord Mayor in 150
years. O'Connell's forecast of the role of a popularly
elected local government body in nationalist agitation
proved correct. After O'Connell's great Repeal debate
in the Dublin Corporation in March 1843 Liberal-
dominated corporations and town councils in Sligo,
Drogheda, Galway, Limerick, Longford, Cork, Waterford and other places supported Repeal (VII, 3006).

At the local level the O'Connellite activists were
now experienced politicians, having come into politics
during the 1820s; a most impressive feature of that
generation is their continuity in local politics despite
the changes in emphasis in the national issues: Eman-

cipation, Reform, Tithes, Repeal and Tenant Right. This endurance suggests that the national issues were perceived as umbrella terms for a continuous advance by the Catholic or democratic movement led by O'Connell. The legacy of O'Connellite politics must be assessed with this constancy, both of the local activists and their mode of operation, in mind. The drive for greater Catholic power and control over local affairs was perhaps the strongest force behind O'Connellism. Local patronage, jobs and status fell to Catholics, which together with the promotion of Irish manufacture, tenant-right and resistance to poor rate made Repeal very practical politics. O'Connell united the urban middle class and the tenant farmers behind Repeal. The note of national regeneration which accompanied Repeal was strengthened by the great Temperance Movement led by Father Mathew which O'Connell shrewdly incorporated into the Repeal campaign. The popular outlook tended to see Temperance and Repeal in the same light — as 'the cause' of the people.

The Repeal agitation of the 1840s was a massive expression of popular pressure politics during a period of Tory rule. O'Connell did not expect to obtain Repeal in the British parliament but he did intend to keep the Irish Question at the centre of British politics in the belief that this would eventually involve a devolution of power to an Irish legislature. By the summer of 1843 he had forced Peel to construct a new Irish policy and to come forward with new measures of reform. This Tory conversion was the most immediate and obvious achievement of the Repeal Association.

4

In 1830 Thomas Attwood sought O'Connell's advice when forming the Birmingham Political Union and

O'Connell outlined his political methodology for
[116] 'attaining constitutional objects'. There were two
principal means:

> The first is the perpetual determination to avoid
> anything like physical force or violence and by
> keeping in all respects within the letter as well
> as the spirit of the law, to continue peaceable,
> rational, but energetic measures so as to combine
> the wise and the good of all classes, stations and
> persuasions in one determination . . . The other is
> to obtain funds by the extension of a plan of collec-
> tion which shall *accept* from no man more than he
> can with the utmost facility spare . . . (IV, 1640).

O'Connell's political prescription, deriving from his
experience in the 1820s, shaped not only English Reform organisations and the Anti-Corn Law League
but also his own great Repeal Association of the
1840s. The Repeal Association surpassed any of
O'Connell's previous organisations in sophistication:
by 1845–46 there were between fifty and sixty people
on the staff of the Association and T. M. Ray had it
organised as a model of efficiency in different depart-
ments and committees. The Repeal Association held
weekly meetings in public at its permanent headquar-
ters, Conciliation Hall, which it built in 1843 on
Burgh Quay, Dublin; a hierarchy of membership
descended from Volunteers to Members to Associate
Members and these were formed into local branches.
A network of Repeal wardens supervised local repeal
reading-rooms and acted as local collectors of the
Repeal Rent.

The Repeal Association quickly surpassed all previous Irish political movements in terms of sophisticated central organisation in Dublin and ability to
mobilise at mass meetings. Subsequent Irish political
parties such as Parnell's and de Valera's succeeded

better in terms of local organisation but did not approach the scale of central organisation or mobilising power of the Repeal Association, at least in terms of public demonstrations so soon after foundation. Ray's Memorandum on the establishment and mode of conducting business in the Repeal Association could be read with profit by every modern party secretary (*16*, II, 160–81). The Repeal Rent rose from £2,688 in 1840 to £8,685 in 1841, declined slightly while O'Connell was Lord Mayor to £5,705 but rose dramatically to £48,706 in 1843, £43,884 in 1844 before falling to £17,824 in 1845 (*76*, 121).

O'Connell's second principal condition for an effective organisation was met with these funds; the first was attempted through a range of experiments to combine the people 'in one determination'. The most impressive of these were the 'monster' meetings held at about thirty centres during the summer and autumn of 1843 in Connaught, Leinster and Munster. According to O'Connell at Drogheda in June 1843 the purpose of these meetings was not to convince Irish opinion of Repeal

> but to convince our enemies – to convince the British statesmen – to make the Duke of Wellington aware of it, bothered as the poor old man is *(loud laughter)*. I want to make all Europe and America know it – I want to make England feel her weakness if she refuses to give the justice we require – the restoration of our domestic parliament . . . If those meetings don't procure something I am bound to do something substantial, and the basis of the movement to affect that object is to be found in those meetings. They are satisfying both friends and foes that the nation is with me – man for man with man – aye, and ready if it were necessary, to perish to the last man *(the entire company arose, and continued cheering for several minutes)*.[3]

Similarly at Longford in May O'Connell again used [118] very ambiguous language:

> We will put them in the wrong, and if a civil war should take place it must be of their making — We shall not be in the slightest degree in fault, for we will not violate any law whatever, and I tell you what, if they attack us, then — *(The hon. and learned gentleman here slapped his breast warmly, midst the most enthusiastic peals of acclamation)* Who will then be the coward? *(renewed cheers)* . . . You will fight for Repeal and liberty; go home quietly, tell your friends of this day's news and when I want you again I'll let you know the day.[4]

O'Connell's defiant attitude was also clearly expressed in Mallow on 11 June when he declared that Irishmen would soon have the alternative of 'living as slaves' or 'dying as freemen' and he indicated that he favoured resistance if Peel and Wellington made 'war on the Irish people'. These militant speeches, especially the 'Mallow Defiance', had a definite place in O'Connell's strategy: they were intended to convey to the government the inadvisability of repression and coercion and the advisability of concession. The government had dismissed twenty-four magistrates for attending Repeal meetings and was threatening to resist the demand for Repeal by force. O'Connell's massive mobilisation of the people in 1843 — between three and four millions may have attended these 'monster' meetings — was the pinnacle of his career as a popular leader. There is an impressive grandeur about O'Connell that summer as he toured Ireland with a vigour which belied his old age:

> There was no rival to his supremacy — there was no restriction to his authority. He played with the fierce enthusiasm he had aroused with the negli-

gent ease of a master; he governed the complicated organisation he had created with a sagacity that rarely failed. He had made himself the focus of the attention of other lands, and the centre around which most of the rising intellect of his own revolved (*35*, 138–9).

The experiment of the 'monster' meetings was accompanied by other novel techniques of extra-parliamentary agitation, some of which were to have a profound influence on later Irish nationalist movements. O'Connell announced plans for a Council of Three Hundred which would prepare for an Irish House of Commons and form a *de facto* and provisional Irish government. This announcement was accompanied by the adoption of a plan to by-pass the normal courts of law by setting up local arbitration courts to be used on a voluntary basis. These plans contained the germs of later Sinn Féin policy. In August and September 1843 O'Connell hinted at a policy of passive resistance to a British effort to destroy Repeal. This would include economic non-co-operation and the creation of chaos generally but he never fully explored this policy. He closed off the radical agrarian option proposed by William Connor which involved non-payment of rent, tithe rent-charge, court cess or any charge out of land until Repeal was granted. A small no rent agitation in Co. Carlow was ignored. He did not attempt to link up the British and Irish struggles in any coherent way, though he supported the Anti-Corn Law League, and he did not seek to exploit to the fullest extent French and American support. He delayed calling the Council of Three Hundred because of the legal dangers involved and finally he called off the last 'monster' meeting at Clontarf in October when the government proclaimed it.

The political assessment made by O'Connell was [120] influenced mainly by the parliamentary situation. Well before Clontarf he was expecting the Whig leaders to begin exploiting Irish agitation to topple the Tories (VII, 3034). In September O'Connell observed that the 'stage coach of the constitution was going down hill too rapidly' and found it necessary to act as 'a drag upon the wheels'.[5] He was preparing for a long, patient, struggle and an eventual renewal of the Whig alliance.

By late 1843 Peel had decided upon a two-pronged Irish policy: a crack-down on agitation followed by an extensive programme of reforms. The show-down necessitated by the first prong came in October 1843. O'Connell's climax to his great popular mobilisation of the people behind Repeal, the Clontarf monster meeting on 8 October, was frustrated when the meeting was banned and armed troops were positioned to prevent it taking place. O'Connell immediately obeyed the proclamation; he had seen already by September that new tactics were needed and he had begun the readjustment to the parliamentary scene.

The 1843 campaign had failed because it was based on a false assumption. The Repeal cause, unlike Emancipation, had no support in Britain and Peel could contemplate military suppression, which would have been impossible in 1828. Repeal seemed to strike at the very heart of the British Empire and to question the assumptions of superiority held by British imperialists, just as Home Rule was to do in subsequent decades. O'Connell expected, on his Emancipation experience, too much from his policy of brinkmanship.

After the submission to the government proclamation on Clontarf O'Connell, his son John, T. M. Ray, Thomas Steele, Charles Gavan Duffy, John Gray, Richard Barrett and two priests were charged with conspiring to obtain by unlawful methods a change in the constitution and government of the country. [121] The trial commenced in January 1844 and ended in February in a verdict of guilty. On 30 May O'Connell was sentenced to one year in jail and a fine of £2,000 and his associates to nine months imprisonment. O'Connell was imprisoned in Richmond Bridewell in comfortable apartments and relatively easy visiting conditions were granted. On appeal to the House of Lords the judgment was reversed in early September and the prisoners released.

The great trial, which cost the Repeal Association £50,000, the strain of analysing his 'monster' meetings and speeches before the all-Protestant jury and finally the imprisonment drained O'Connell's 'nerve power', to use Gladstone's phrase. He was just turning seventy and had completed one of the most strenuous years in his long career of agitation. O'Connell managed to stage some impressive theatricalism during the trial and the release; his dramatic gesture towards the College Green parliament buildings was to be repeated by Parnell. He was, however, clearly an old man when he was released.

5

In the autumn of 1841 Charles Gavan Duffy, editor of the *Belfast Vindicator,* a Catholic pro-O'Connell paper, met John Blake Dillon and Thomas Davis, both products of Trinity College, Dublin. The three became close political friends and resolved to establish a new nationalist newspaper in Dublin. *The Nation* first appeared in October 1842. It was clear from the beginning that a new concept of nationalism lay behind *The Nation* because it sought, as well as self-government, to 'influence and purify' the people with a comprehensive nationality which had at its

centre an intense emotional conviction which made
[122] an absolute demand for the independence of the Irish
nation. This new, uncompromising attitude amongst
the young men in Dublin who associated with *The
Nation* group did not have any divisive effect on the
debates in the Repeal Association until 1844. There
was a great deal of common ground between these
Young Irelanders, as they were styled, and O'Connell.
They readily accepted O'Connell's leadership and
general aims and contributed a great deal to the
enthusiasm and flair of the 1843 campaign. *The
Nation* fully supported O'Connell's policy on obeying
the Clontarf proclamation and the later criticisms of
Gavan Duffy and others on 'the Clontarf surrender'
hide the fact that they agreed with O'Connell at
the time.

While O'Connell was in prison he handed over
management of the Repeal Association to William
Smith O'Brien, a Protestant landlord MP, who had
recently announced his Repeal conversion. O'Connell
valued Davis and Smith O'Brien as evidence of the
attractiveness of Repeal for reasonable and fair-
minded Protestants: he had always hoped to unite
the different creeds in Ireland behind his programme.
This interlude in 1844 brought the Young Irelanders
closer to the centre of the Repeal Association as, in
the absence of O'Connell and his son John, Davis and
Smith O'Brien got on very well together as leaders of
the Association.

Davis was an attractive and able young patriot but
he had a strain of self-righteousness and a pugnacious
quality which soon led to an estrangement with
O'Connell. The Young Irelanders tended towards an
extravagant, romantic response to politics and pro-
fessed contempt for moderation and compromise, in
the manner of many young radicals. Compromise,
however, in the shape of O'Connell, commanded an

unrivalled degree of public support. Nevertheless, Young Ireland gradually began to disparage the political morality of O'Connell's actions. Davis felt that the Repeal Association lent far too much towards a Catholic view and that O'Connell encouraged 'Catholic bigotry'. This was especially the case when newspapers, possibly jealous of *The Nation*, such as *The Pilot*, attacked it when the opportunity arose. Davis felt O'Connell could and should be able to prevent these attacks. He also disliked aspects of O'Connell's leadership such as his absolute control over Repeal funds, his abusive language and some of his policies, for example, in education.

The relationships within the Repeal Association were soon put under pressure by Peel's reform measures brought forward to kill Repeal through 'kindness'; at least 'kindness' to the Catholic Church and middle class. Peel introduced a Charitable Donations and Bequests Bill in June 1844 which appeared to be an advance for Catholics, as it abolished the old Protestant-controlled board and gave Catholics five places on a smaller board. It also gave some legal recognition to Catholic bishops in Ireland. However, it cast reflection upon the honesty of purpose of the Irish clergy in some clauses and appeared to prejudice the position of religious orders. Archbishop MacHale launched a full-scale attack on the bill and this was followed by O'Connell's critical response. MacHale and O'Connell appeared to Davis to be taking it for granted that the Repeal Association was in practice a Catholic organisation.

In October 1844 O'Connell, seeking to obtain wider support for the Repeal Association, indicated a possible retreat from the full programme of the Association when he wooed the Irish federalists. Greatly alarmed, the Young Irelanders attempted to force O'Connell back on to the straight-and-narrow

of 'simple Repeal'. A very rancorous atmosphere
[124] developed. Davis, extremely sensitive about the place
of Protestants in a self-governing Ireland, resented
O'Connell's political manoeuvres (VII, 3109).

This was the background when Peel introduced the
Colleges Bill in May 1845. The Young Irelanders
supported the bill because they believed secular and
mixed denominational education would lead towards
a comprehensive nationality. They underestimated
the significance and strength of the opposition in
Catholic circles to combined university education for
Catholics and Protestants. To many Catholics the new
colleges under Peel's bill appeared to be 'godless' and
to the extreme MacHale it was an 'infidel and slavish
and demoralising scheme'. However, a minority of the
Catholic bishops tended towards acceptance of the
proposal. O'Connell would have supported mixed
education with provision for separate religious education but he had already conceded to the Catholic
Church the right to control the education of Catholics.
O'Connell's experience of sectarian influences in Irish
education went back a number of decades to his
conflicts with the Kildare Place Society, which had
been suspected of proselytism. Defence of Catholic
education had been a prime plank in the platform of
the Catholic Association.

The young men supporting Davis were now up
against the party machine and O'Connell's unrivalled
popularity and it is easy to sense the tension when
O'Connell and Davis openly clashed in the Repeal
Association on 26 May 1845. Davis very cleverly
attempted to show that Catholic bishops accepted
the principle of 'mixed' education, which was a
plausible misinterpretation of the profound distrust
of the bill amongst most bishops. O'Connell was
infuriated and denounced Young Ireland; his outburst
was the product of previous personal criticism and

innuendo from Davis and *The Nation* group. Davis, nervous and exhausted, burst into tears, giving O'Connell the opportunity to effect a public reconciliation, declaring dramatically, 'Davis, I love you'.

Between O'Connell and Young Ireland there soon appeared wide differences on nationalism, education and religion, the conduct of the Association and democracy. O'Connell's democratic stance alarmed the conservative Young Irelanders like Smith O'Brien (*81*, 89). When Davis died in September 1845 the Young Ireland group lost their most able advocate and the rift between Young and Old Ireland widened considerably.

The sudden failure in the late autumn of 1845 of the greater part of the potato crop confronted Ireland with the near certainty of famine. O'Connell at once grasped the full extent of the disaster. In October he set up the Mansion House Committee in Dublin which included Whigs and Repealers. In November he led a deputation from this committee to the Lord Lieutenant to demand the immediate stoppage of all exports of corn and provisions, the opening of the ports for the import of food, the setting up of relief machinery and food stores in all counties and the provision of employment on useful public works funded by a tax on landlords and a government loan. The cold government reception to these proposals helped to confirm O'Connell in his belief that the Tories would not deal generously with the extremely grave situation. O'Connell set this out clearly to Smith O'Brien in December 1845 when arguing that Repealers could not observe a 'strict neutrality' between Whigs and Tories in the Commons as Young Irelanders and Smith O'Brien suggested. O'Connell's clear duty, he felt, was to 'squeeze out' a great deal of good for Ireland 'without for one moment merging or even postponing Repeal but on the contrary advancing that measure' (VII, 3180, 3181). In fact Young Ireland paid little or no attention to what should be done to avert famine in 1845—46 (*81*, 98—9). O'Connell realised that the lives of the Irish people depended upon the ability of the government to respond to the crisis. The centre of action had reverted to Westminster.

6

During the political crisis of December 1845 caused by Peel's espousal of Corn Law abolition O'Connell was ready to support both the Whigs and the repeal of the Corn Laws. To the Young Irelanders the repeal of the Corn Laws was at least an 'open question' for the nationalist movement but the Whig alliance appeared to them to be a complete abandonment of their absolute ideal. O'Connell, however, felt he could not afford the luxury of absolutes: 'How', he asked, 'can we insist upon the Government finding employment and food . . . if we vote in favour of the Corn Laws and thereby prevent food from being as cheap as it would otherwise be? How can we on the one hand complain of starvation and on the other vote against provisions being as cheap as they might otherwise be?' (VII, 3181). There was a case for Irish protectionism but he felt this was not the time to make it. O'Connell hoped to get not only substantial famine relief from the Whigs but extensive reforms as well. He had increasingly focused on tenant-right. It is significant that when he dismissed many suggested Whig bills in April 1845 as 'whistling jigs to mile-stones' the 'substantial' measures he sought included mainly land reforms — a large absentee tax, 'tenant-right, confirmed by law as far as it ought to be sanctioned', compensation for improvements and the taking away of the power of distraining; he argued that 'the occupying tenant' was 'the Hamlet left out by special desire' from the Devon Land Commission [127] Report: 'He must be relieved, or depend upon it, depend upon it, he will go mad' (VII, 3141).

O'Connell devoted his time to the parliamentary sessions in London in 1846. He opposed the Coercion Bill which the government had introduced to deal with famine-stricken Ireland. From the end of March, with a following of fifty Repealers and Liberals, O'Connell fought a long and successful delaying action against the Coercion Bill. Peel's comments are revealing in June 1846:

> There is an Irish party, a determined and not insignificant one, for which British indignation has no terrors. Their wish is to disgust England with Irish business and with Irish members, and to induce England ... to listen to a repeal of the Legislative Union for the purpose of purging the House of a set of troublesome and factious members who equally obstruct legislation for Ireland and for Great Britain (*76*, 287–8).

Peel's government was finally defeated by a combination of Whigs, O'Connellites and Tory Protectionists. O'Connell was now in clear alliance with Lord John Russell's new government. He had made 'great and despairing' efforts in major speeches in February and April 1846 to bring home the real extent of the disaster in Ireland to parliament. He was over seventy years of age and presented in Disraeli's words

> a strange and touching spectacle to those who remembered the form of colossal energy and the clear and thrilling tones which had once startled, disturbed and controlled senates. . . . To the house generally it was a performance of dumb show, a feeble old man muttering before a table; but

respect for the great parliamentary personage kept all as orderly as if the fortunes of a party hung upon his rhetoric (*76*, 290).

O'Connell's physical decline became very evident from the time of his imprisonment in 1844; O'Neill Daunt recalled that 'His step was heavy, and the vivacity of his manner had given place to an air of languor. He sometimes went over to a mirror, saying, "Well — I think I am looking very old and worn. I perceive the change in myself very much. I think my face has got a very haggard look"' (*20*, II, 244). O'Connell's political perceptions, however, were still acute. While in London he received regular reports from Thomas Steele, T. M. Ray and others about the behaviour of the Young Ireland group within the Repeal Association. In May 1846 Steele urged that the divisions 'should be brought to a crisis' (VIII, 3207).

What worried Ray and O'Connell especially was the advocacy of physical force (VIII, 3216). This was really serious whereas young Thomas Francis Meagher's criticisms of the Whig alliance could pass as merely irritating and mischievous. O'Connell's men were delighted when he promised to deal with them. As Steele told him, 'It has given your own Old Ireland people joy beyond measure that on your return you intend putting these scamps in their proper position' (VIII, 3228a). When O'Connell returned home he outlined the Irish programme he expected to urge upon the new Whig government. Besides a radical reform of landlord-tenant relations and an absentee tax of 20 per cent O'Connell sought the extension of the suffrage, municipal reform to be comparable to that for England, elected county boards instead of grand juries and education to be developed along denominational lines. O'Connell believed that the

Devon Commission had made radical land reform practical politics for the first time in his life and with the Tory party split he hoped the Whigs could consider his measures. The Repeal Association accepted his proposals and Young Ireland acquiesced in silence. Thus O'Connell's Whig alliance was ensured before he moved to reiterate the pacific nature of the Repeal Association. He introduced a statement on his moral force principles (soon to be known as the 'Peace Resolutions') on 11 July 1846:

> That to promote political amelioration, peaceable means alone should be used, to the exclusion of all others, save those that are peaceable, legal and constitutional. It has been said very unwisely that this principle prohibits the necessary defence against unjust aggression on the part of a domestic government or a foreign enemy. It does no such thing; it leaves the right of self-defence perfectly free to the use of any force sufficient to resist and defeat unjust aggression.

O'Connell sought for the Repeal Association to adopt this statement unequivocally, renouncing physical force as a possible means of securing Repeal should constitutional means fail. He declared that he 'drew up this resolution to draw a marked line between Young Ireland and Old Ireland' but the Association adopted the statement by acclamation, Meagher alone dissenting. O'Connell returned to London having successfully tested 'the first principle' of his political life; he had refused to be 'humbugged' by John Mitchel's 'species of pretended acquiescence and real difference' by declaring that he would expel anyone who violated the Peace Resolutions now that the Association had adopted a clear policy. He was prepared to act with Young Ireland if they candidly retracted their physical-force opinions, as he told

Smith O'Brien, whom he actually asked to come up [130] to Dublin during his absence (VIII, 3248).

On 28 July the Repeal Association had another long debate on the subject of physical as against moral force. When John O'Connell said that any members who refused to accept O'Connell's interpretation of the Peace Resolutions were opposed to O'Connell's leadership, Smith O'Brien, followed by several others, including Mitchel, Meagher and Duffy, walked out. Their action proved to be Young Ireland's secession from the Association. O'Connell's skilful leadership was intended to defeat Young Ireland as an independent force within the Repeal Association and had there been no failure of the potato in the autumn of 1846 the course of politics would probably have confirmed O'Connell's success in July.

After the breach Young Ireland had no policy or organisation and they mostly concentrated upon literary matters (81, 111—12). Attempts at a reconciliation failed in late 1846. In January 1847 they organised the Irish Confederation but it too split. The Young Irelanders proved totally incapable of organising any serious revolution, divorced as they were from social realities in rural Ireland. However, the fumbling inadequacy of the Whig government's relief measures in the famine winter of 1846—47 exposed O'Connell's hopes mercilessly; by December 1846 he was denouncing the Whigs. He became involved in the Reproductive Works Committee composed of MPs and landowners. At a meeting of this body in January 1847 a decision was taken by eighty-three peers and MPs to act together as an Irish party to procure public funds for the 'imperial calamity'. In parliament the fragile unity of this Irish Party was easily shattered and English politicians continued to saddle Irish landlordism with responsibility for Irish conditions. How different it would all have been, O'Connell felt, 'if we had our own parliament, taking care of our people, of our own resources'.

In his last speech, he declared that only 'a great national act of charity' could save the lives of a quarter of the Irish population: 'Food must be procured for the people wherever it could be got, and at whatever expense.' He told the Commons that Ireland 'was in their hands. If they did not save her, she could not save herself'. He saw the nation sinking and was finally overcome by illness, exhaustion and grief. Knowing his death was at hand he set off for Rome, meeting tributes along the way, and he died, in great agony of mind, at Genoa on 15 May 1847 before he reached the spiritual consolation he believed he might find in Rome.

6
Conclusion

History can reach no unchallengeable conclusions on so many-sided a character, on a life so dominated, so profoundly agitated, by the circumstances of the time. For that I bear history no grudge. To expect from history those final conclusions which may perhaps be obtained in other disciplines is in my opinion to misunderstand its nature.[1]

History is an argument without end. There can be no finality in an assessment of O'Connell, as protean a figure as his great contemporary Napoleon. O'Connell's ultimate significance lies in the way he affected the Irish mind and, I hazard, continues to affect it. His work and legend continues to mean different things to different people; as Ventura declared in his great funeral oration on O'Connell: 'God does not create a great man for the use of a single age or a single people.'

O'Connell's personality has attracted as much as it has repelled. Sean O'Faolain describes the almost physical repulsion felt by his opponents in the 1840s to the 'face' they saw in O'Connell. 'It is the face that Young Ireland was to fear and hate, the image that meant to their eager and open hearts everything hateful in the way of cabal and cunning plots, that made them shiver as before everything that would destroy every dream by which they lived' (40, 253). The description owes a great deal to the portrait of O'Connell presented in later years by Young Irelanders such as John Mitchel; however, as Owen Dudley Edwards has pointed out, 'It is as reasonable to [133] accept *Jail Journal's* view of O'Connell as it would be to accept notions on democracy from *Mein Kampf*, its European counterpart'.[2]

That is not to deny that there was a great deal in O'Connell's behaviour about which contemporaries were critical. O'Connell's love of power and his methods of gaining and keeping it were not always scrupulous, and his policy often seemed to be guided by expediency rather than by principle. The note of disillusion was sounded in 1834 by Thomas Moore when he wrote the lines beginning, 'The dream of those days when first I sung thee is o'er'. But this fastidiousness tended to come either from the Tories or from those who were depressed by the brutal realities of Irish life. O'Connell was the leader of the Irish Catholic nation. He did not choose to be a Catholic leader, indeed he passionately wanted a non-sectarian Ireland. But he was a realist. He understood the depth of Irish sectarian divisions and did not baulk at unpalatable measures necessary to advance the cause of the people he led. As Gladstone pointed out: 'this nation, weak, outnumbered, and despised, he led, not always unsuccessfully, in its controversy with another nation, the strongest perhaps and the proudest in Europe'. Young Ireland, on the other hand, was an elite out of touch with political realities and with the people O'Connell led.

O'Connell was subject to confusing extremes in his behaviour: he oscillated between the convinced rationalist and the popular leader whose power depended upon crowds, feelings, and emotions rather than reason. He was an extreme optimist, occasionally to the point of unreality, but he also passed through bouts of great pessimism and even despair. Other extremes are evident: his behaviour when entering parliament — the very model of propriety — contrasted with his indulgence in coarse and vulgar abuse which he himself admitted to be a grave fault. His behaviour depended to a large extent upon his need for approval and applause; Hunting Cap had early recognised O'Connell's disposition to reflect that side of himself which would gain acceptance. Yet O'Connell never sacrificed a vital principle to this propensity, though he sometimes came very close to it, as his London experience of 1825 revealed. However, he never accepted office (only very minor positions were obtained for his own family) and he sought no personal or family advantage from his political manipulations, such as the Whig alliance.

The development of O'Connell's character over many years of political involvement reveals how deeply he was affected by circumstances. He became a symbol for his people; he led them 'by direct personal agency' and the group he led had as big an effect on him as he had on them; while he 'liberated' the people he became himself, in some respects, their captive. Repeal, for example, was raised in the 1840s much more under clerical auspices, much more distinctly as a Catholic expression than the young O'Connell would have wished. It became impossible for him to reconcile the conflicting cultures and identities in Ireland and by the 1830s and 1840s he had been forced to become the leader of the oppressed majority. He inevitably became a bogey-man to Northern Protestants.

O'Connell's greatness emerges in his preservation of his liberal Catholic beliefs when sectarian pressures seemed so overpowering. In an unequal situation he struggled to ensure that in a self-governing Ireland there would be 'perfect religious freedom', 'perfect freedom of conscience for *all* and for *every* one' (VII, 3116). He was a victim of the sectarian circumstances in which he had to struggle for religious and civil equality for the majority of the Irish people. He [135] always maintained the necessity for conciliation, declaring to the Repeal Association in March 1843 that 'The man who can conciliate a single Protestant, Presbyterian, or unwilling Catholic, is, to my mind, the best of patriots . . . Perhaps it may be said that I am an unfit person . . . I must admit that during the contest for Emancipation I have often used scathing and violent words . . .'

O'Connell justified this behaviour by showing the abuse to which he had been subjected. As symbol of his country, he was also a victim of British prejudice against the Irish Catholics. In 1839 he writes to T. M. Ray on such attitudes:

There is an utter ignorance of, and indifference to, our sufferings and privations. It is really idle to expect that it could be otherwise! What care they for us, provided we be submissive, pay the taxes, furnish recruits for the Army and Navy and bless the masters who either despise or oppress or combine both? The apathy that exists respecting Ireland is worse than the national antipathy they bear us (VI, 2588).

The British 'apathy and antipathy' convinced O'Connell that for Ireland to have good government it would have to have self-government. He told Bishop Doyle in 1831: 'No person knows better than you do that the domination of England is the sole and blighting curse of this country. It is the incubus that sits on our energies, stops the pulsation of the nation's heart and leaves to Ireland not gay vitality but the horrid convulsions of a troubled dream' (IV, 1860). O'Connell realised that the rhythm and pattern of Irish public life was being continuously distorted through forced conformity to quite different impulses in Britain. He wished to restore the national and public life of Ireland which had been 'not only enfeebled, but exhausted and paralysed by the Act of Union' (*59*, 155).

O'Connell was in the messianic tradition of political leadership although he was as much 'prophet' as Messiah. The illusion that any one great leader can be the deliverer of a people was shattered in the 1840s, but the cult of leadership persisted in Ireland beyond Parnell to de Valera. In the end, O'Connell the Messiah was rendered impotent by the catastrophe of the Famine. O'Connell simply could not bear, in Gladstone's words, 'his own heart-rending sense of incapacity' to relieve his people.

He had quickly seen the deadly effects of the Famine and had reacted more swiftly and with greater insight than the literary Young Irelanders, who subsequently accused O'Connell of being some sort of 'magician' who 'bewitched' the Irish people to their destruction. Yet Mitchel admitted that in 1847 the Irish Confederation 'had no much clearer view through the gloom' than Conciliation Hall (*12*, xv–xix). Lecky observed there was 'something almost awful in so dark a close of so brilliant a career'. The 'awfulness' arises in large part from the failure of the British parliament to respond to Irish needs in the years after the Union. There can be little doubt that had Ireland had a domestic parliament, with O'Connell as Prime Minister, the prevailing economic orthodoxies would have given way to the needs of the people.

The evidence for this is two-fold: firstly, the economic policies advocated by O'Connell, as we have seen, departed from laissez-faire principles in a fundamental fashion. O'Connell was prepared to go 'all against the doctrines of political economy' when the circumstances of the country required it.[3]

Secondly, the poverty of Irish Catholics determined the welfare-oriented machine politics which was particularly O'Connell's creation. O'Connellite organisations dealt with and resolved grievances as far as possible. T. M. Ray estimated that between £30,000 and £40,000 was given as grants in 'grievance cases' by the Repeal Association (*16*, II, 174). The Catholic Association had inaugurated this welfare-oriented style of politics, which is best seen in operation at local level, where it was necessary to spend great sums of money to combat the economic dominance of the landlords. In Co. Waterford in 1826 the O'Connellite Committee provided alternative employment and even built houses for the people. As one priest put it succinctly: *'Patriotism may fill a man's heart, but cannot fill the belly'.*[4]

There was a socio-economic imperative in O'Connellite politics which has been quite undervalued in subsequent analyses. Abstract theory was never O'Connell's forte. In practice, O'Connellism was a social reform movement: Catholic communalism was more powerful than laissez-faire liberalism. This was also the case with Catholic 'boss politics' in the United States which owed a great deal to O'Connellism. O'Connell's sympathies for the economically oppressed together with his knowledge of Irish conditions was the basis for his reform proposals. Repeal was no panacea for Irish problems but, had it come in time, it would have made the solution of the problems easier: a reformed Irish parliament would have been more responsive to Irish needs. Even without Repeal O'Connell's identification of government responsibility to reform the land system, to aid Irish manufactures, to aid emigrants, to control the food supply in emergencies and to aid productive public works would have done much to minimise the suffering of the people. The British government proved unable to meet its responsibility assumed through the Act of Union.

O'Connell's nationality had an indispensable quality of universalism and a deep commitment to human rights and liberation which Irish nationalism was the poorer for ignoring while under the spell of writers such as Mitchel, Griffith and Pearse. Racial exclusiveness and the subjection of culture to politics revolted O'Connell. The clash between Young Ireland and O'Connell was the first classic encounter between an Irish nationalism founded upon democracy and good government and a nationalism constructed by literary men in mystical and cultural terms. Young Ireland cultural nationalism looked back to an ancient Irish civilisation with its own language, literature and history and sought its re-creation by a revolution which would abolish not only English sovereignty but also the more subtle domination of English culture. Ultimately cultural nationalism made of the Irish language a political weapon. O'Connell, believing in cultural freedom and universalist values, left the Irish language free of political content. It is perhaps futile to speculate whether in an independent Ireland composed of conflicting cultures and identities the O'Connellite approach would have left the language in a better position to gain widespread acceptance; certainly the end product of cultural nationalism was to make the language seem the property of one group on the island.

Gaelic Ireland, as a community of people from whom O'Connell sprang and with whom he lived, did not see revival of the Irish language as part of O'Connell's political obligation. His own pragmatic attitude reflected that of Irish speakers generally. O'Connell was loved and honoured by Gaelic Ireland. He was the hero who combated the Protestant agents of oppression encountered by the Catholic, Irish-speaking, peasantry (*96*, 31–2). He was certainly not indifferent to Gaelic culture in which he revelled in Kerry; his personality was moulded within that culture. He was, however, in favour of anglicisation as an essential part of Irish liberation, viewing language through the eyes of an eighteenth-century, Enlightenment universalist. He was an avid reader of romantic literature and was much attached to Thomas Moore's melodies, which gave public dignity to an ancient Irish tradition. Moore was the most popular Irish cultural figure in O'Connell's day. In the first half of the nineteenth century, Europe began to perceive a distinctive Ireland emerging, moulded by the poetry of Moore and the politics of O'Connell.

O'Connell hated both racism and militarism; he was not a pacifist, believing that a country had a right to resist aggression and to defend itself. However, O'Connell believed that Irish violence would amount to either a sectarian bloodletting, as in 1798, or to a farcical revolution, as in 1848. He belongs to that small band of men, which includes Gandhi and Martin Luther King, who have expanded the range of techniques which can be used by the oppressed and excluded to advance politically. O'Connell would defend liberty, and in certain circumstances pursue it by military means but he believed that the conditions for a just war simply did not obtain in Ireland. Irish divisions, religious, racial and economic, meant that revolutionary violence would degenerate and would be bound to fail; it could not unite all groups and bring forth a real Irish liberation.

> The principle of my political life and that in which I have instructed the people of Ireland is, that all ameliorations and improvements in political institutions can be obtained by persevering in a perfectly peaceable and legal course, and cannot be obtained

by forcible means, *or if they could be got by forcible means, such means create more evils than they cure, and leave the county worse than they found it.*[5]

Such principles prevent O'Connell passing out of 'the mill-stream of politics into the domain of history' which Gladstone incorrectly assumed he had done by 1889. Michael Davitt's summary of O'Connell's achievement can hardly be surpassed:

Ireland has never produced a greater man than O'Connell, and Europe very few that can truly be called his equal in the work of uplifting a people from the degrading status of religious and political serfdom to conditions of national life which necessarily created changes and chances of progress that were bound to lead on to the gain of further liberty (*53*, 35).

References

Chapter 1: 'The Grand Theatre of the World' (pp. 4—13)
1. Lecture to O'Connell Folk School, Derrynane, 17 August 1975, quoted in *The Irish Times*, 18 August 1975.

Chapter 2: 'The Man of the People' (pp. 14—40)
1. I have traced in some detail the emergence of Irish liberal Catholicism as a political ideology in my Ph.D. thesis: R. F. B. O'Ferrall, *The Growth of Political Consciousness in Ireland 1823—1847: A Study of O'Connellite Politics and Political Education*, Trinity College, Dublin 1978, 101—57.
2. William Parnell to Denys Scully, 3 December 1811, Scully Papers (to be deposited in the National Library of Ireland); I am most grateful to Professor M. R. O'Connell for bringing this remarkable letter to my notice.

Chapter 3: 'A Bloodless Revolution' (pp. 41—67)
1. Report of meeting, 27 February 1824, State Paper Office, Dublin, Catholic Association Papers.
2. *Parliamentary Debates*, New Series, XII, 15 February 1825, Col. 465.
3. *Dublin Evening Post*, 27 April 1826.
4. R. F. B. O'Ferrall, *The Growth of Political Consciousness in Ireland 1823—1847: A Study of O'Connellite Politics and Political Education*, Ph.D. thesis, TCD 1978, 269.
5. Report of meeting, 16 December 1824, State Paper Office, Dublin, Catholic Association Papers.
6. Report of meeting, 8 January 1825, State Paper Office, Dublin, Catholic Association Papers.
7. Letter of Rev. Thomas Moylan, P.P., probably to O'Connell, 23 November 1826, Catholic Proceedings, Archbishop's House, Dublin.
8. *Dublin Evening Post*, 6 June 1826.

9. *Dublin Evening Post,* 19 April 1828.

[142] 10. This placard survives in Catholic Proceedings, Archbishop's House, Dublin.

11. D. O'Connell, *Seven Letters on the Reform Bill and the Law of Elections in Ireland,* Dublin 1835, which reprints O'Connell's public letters to *The Pilot* in 1832.

Chapter 4: 'Justice or Repeal' (pp. 68—103)

1. *Dublin Evening Post,* 28 May 1829.
2. *Hansard,* New Series, XIII, 793 (23 March 1830).
3. *Hansard,* New Series, XXII, 93—97 (4 February 1830); *ibid,* 3rd Series, I, 327 (9 November 1830).
4. *Hansard,* 3rd Series, I, 327 (9 November 1830).
5. *Hansard,* 3rd Series, XV, 160 (5 February 1833).
6. *Hansard,* 3rd Series, IV, 652—3 (4 July 1831).
7. *Hansard,* New Series, XXII, 93—97 (4 February 1830).
8. *Hansard,* 3rd Series, I, 321—5 (9 November 1830).
9. *Hansard,* 3rd Series, XXII, 1282 (22 April 1834); 272 (29 April 1834).
10. *Letter from the Rev. Henry Montgomery to Daniel O'Connell, Esq, M.P.,* Dublin 1831.
11. *The Repealer Repulsed! A Correct Narrative of the Rise and Progress of the Repeal Invasion of Ulster: Dr. Cooke's Challenge and Mr. O'Connell's declinature, tactics and flight,* Belfast 1841, 12, 110.
12. *Hansard,* 3rd Series, XV, 148—77 (5 February 1833).
13. *Hansard,* 3rd Series, XXXI, 98 (4 February 1836).
14. *Hansard,* New Series, XIII, 793 (23 March 1830).
15. *Hansard,* 3rd Series, I, 377—8 (11 November 1830).
16. *Hansard,* 3rd Series, XL, 1084—97 (13 February 1838).

Chapter 5: 'A Prophet of a Coming Time' (pp. 104—131)

1. Daniel O'Connell to the Cincinnati Irish Repeal Association, 11 October 1843, published in William Lloyd Garrison's newspaper, *The Liberator,* 17 November 1843.
2. *Evidence Taken before Commissioners of Inquiry into the State of the Law and Practice in Respect to the Occupation of Land in Ireland,* 1845, Vol. XXI, pp. 933—42.
3. *Freeman's Journal,* 1 July 1843.
4. *The Longford Journal,* 3 June 1843.
5. *The Pilot,* 27 September 1843.

Chapter 6: Conclusion (pp. 132—140)

1. Pieter Geyl, *Napoleon: For and Against,* 1949; Penguin ed., 1976.

2. O. Dudley Edwards, 'A Daniel Come to Judgement', *The Irish Times*, 25 October 1980.

3. O'Connell's evidence to Devon Commission in 1845, see *Evidence Taken Before Commissioners of Inquiry into the State of the Law and Practice in respect to the Occupation of Land in Ireland*, 1845, Vol. XXI, p. 939.

4. Rev. R. Murphy to W. Barron, 31 May 1826, Wyse Papers, National Library of Ireland MS 15,023(4) (emphasis in original).

5. *The Nation*, 18 November 1843 (my italics).

Bibliography

Printed Correspondence and Speeches

1. Cusack, M. F., *Speeches and Public Letters of the Liberator*, 2 vols, Dublin 1875
2. Fitzpatrick, W. J., ed., *Correspondence of Daniel O'Connell*, 2 vols, London 1888
3. O'Connell, J., ed., *The Life and Speeches of Daniel O'Connell*, 2 vols, Dublin 1846
4. O'Connell, J., ed., *The Select Speeches of Daniel O'Connell*, 2 vols, Dublin 1854
5. O'Connell, M. R., ed., *The Correspondence of Daniel O'Connell*, vols I—VIII: vols I—II, Shannon 1972; vols III—VIII, Dublin 1973—80

Memoirs, Works by Daniel O'Connell, Journals and Contemporary Works

6. *A Full and Revised Report of the Three Days' Discussion in the Corporation of Dublin on the Repeal of the Union*, Dublin 1843
7. de Beaumont, G., *L'Irlande, Sociale, Politique et Religieuse*, 2 vols, Paris 1839 (translated and abridged W. Cooke Taylor, 2 vols, London 1839)
8. Houston, A., *Daniel O'Connell: His Early Life, and Journal, 1795 to 1802*, London 1906
9. *Letter from the Rev. Henry Montgomery to Daniel O'Connell, Esq., M.P.*, Dublin 1831
10. MacCabe, W. B., *The Last Days of O'Connell*, Dublin 1847
11. Madden, D. O., *Ireland and Its Rulers Since 1829*, 3 vols, London 1843—44
12. Mitchel, J., *Jail Journal*, Dublin 1864
13. O'Connell, D., *Memoir on Ireland, Native and Saxon, 1172—1660*, I, Dublin 1843
14. O'Connell, D., *Observations on Corn Laws, On Political Pravity and Ingratitude, and on Clerical and Personal*

Slander in the Shape of a Meek and Modest Reply to the Second Letter of the Earl of Shrewsbury, Dublin 1842

15. O'Connell, D., *Seven Letters on the Reform Bill and the Law of Elections in Ireland*, Dublin 1835

16. O'Connell, J., *Recollections and Experiences during a Parliamentary Career from 1833 to 1848*, 2 vols London 1849

17. O'Connell, M. J., *The Last Colonel of the Irish Brigade*, 2 vols, London 1892

18. O'Neill Daunt, W. J., *A Life Spent for Ireland: Selections from the Journals of W. J. O'Neill Daunt*, new ed., Shannon 1972

19. O'Neill Daunt, W. J., *Ireland and Her Agitators*, London 1867

20. O'Neill Daunt, W. J., *Personal Recollections of the Late Daniel O'Connell, M.P.*, 2 vols, London 1848

21. Redding, C., *Past Celebrities Whom I have Known*, II, London 1866

22. Tait, W., *Ireland and O'Connell*, Edinburgh 1835

23. *The Repealer Repulsed! A Correct Narrative of the Rise and Progress of the Repeal Invasion of Ulster*, Belfast 1841

24. Venedey, J., *Ireland and the Irish During the Repeal Year 1843*, trans. W. B. MacCabe, Dublin 1844

25. Wyse, T., *Historical Sketch of the Late Catholic Association of Ireland*, 2 vols, London 1829

Biographies of Daniel O'Connell

26. A Munster Farmer, *Reminiscences of Daniel O'Connell, Esq., M.P., During the Agitations of the Veto, Emancipation and Repeal*, Dublin 1847

27. Cusack, M. F., *The Liberator: His Life and Times*, London 1872

28. Dunlop, R., *Daniel O'Connell and the Revival of National Life in Ireland*, New York 1900

29. Fagan, W., *The Life and Times of Daniel O'Connell*, 2 vols, Cork 1847—48

30. Gondon, J., *Biographie de Daniel O'Connell*, Paris 1847

31. Gwynn, D., *Daniel O'Connell: the Irish Liberator*, London 1929, rev. ed., Cork 1947

32. Hamilton, J. A., *Life of Daniel O'Connell*, London 1888

33. Horgan, J. J., *Great Catholic Laymen: Daniel O'Connell*, Dublin 1905

34. Huish, Robert, *Memoirs Private and Political of Daniel O'Connell,* London 1836
35. Lecky, W. E. H., *The Leaders of Public Opinion in Ireland,* II, new ed., London 1903
36. Luby, T. C., *The Life, Opinions, Conversations and Eloquence of Daniel O'Connell,* New York 1872
37. MacDonagh, M., *Daniel O'Connell and the Story of Catholic Emancipation,* Dublin 1929
38. MacDonagh, M., *The Life of Daniel O'Connell,* London 1903
39. Moley, R., *Daniel O'Connell: Nationalism Without Violence,* New York 1974
40. O'Faolain, S., *King of the Beggars: A Life of Daniel O'Connell,* London 1938, new ed., Dublin 1970
41. O'Keeffe, C. M., *Life and Times of Daniel O'Connell,* Dublin 1864
42. O'Kelly, J. J., *O'Connell Calling: the Liberator's Place in the World,* Tralee 1947
43. O'Rourke, J., *The Centenary Life of O'Connell,* Dublin 1875
44. *The Life and Times of Daniel O'Connell, M.P., With the Beauties of His Principal Speeches,* Dublin 1846

Special Studies and Articles
45. Broderick, J. F., 'The Holy See and the Irish Movement for the Repeal of the Act of Union with England 1829—47', *Analecta Gregoriana* IV, Rome 1951
46. Brown, T. N., 'Nationalism and the Irish Peasant 1800—1848', *The Review of Politics* XV, 1953
47. Cahill, M., 'The 1826 General Election in County Monaghan', *Clogher Record* V, 1964
48. Clarke R., 'The Relations between O'Connell and the Young Irelanders', *Irish Historical Studies* III, 1942
49. Collison Black, R. D., *Economic Thought and the Irish Question 1817—1870,* Cambridge 1960
50. Connolly, J., *Labour in Irish History,* Dublin 1910
51. Cunningham, T. P., 'The 1826 General Election in County Cavan', *Breifne* II, 1962
52. D'Arcy, F. A., 'The Artisans of Dublin and Daniel O'Connell, 1830—47: an unquiet liaison', *Irish Historical Studies* XVII, 1970
53. Davitt, M., *The Fall of Feudalism in Ireland,* London 1904

54. Dudley Edwards, O., 'The American Image of Ireland: a study of its early phases', *Perspectives in American History* IV, Harvard 1970

55. Dudley Edwards, R., *Daniel O'Connell and His World*, London 1975

56. Gash, N., *Mr. Secretary Peel*, London 1961

57. Gavan Duffy, C., *Four Years of Irish History 1845—49*, London 1883

58. Gavan Duffy, C., *Young Ireland, A fragment of History 1840—45*, London 1880

59. Gladstone, W. E., 'Daniel O'Connell', *The Nineteenth Century* XXV, 1889

60. Graham, A. H., 'The Lichfield House Compact, 1835', *Irish Historical Studies* XII, 1961

61. Griffith, F., 'Contemporary Opinion of O'Connell's Oratory', *Eire-Ireland* VII, 1973

62. Gwynn, D., *Daniel O'Connell and Ellen Courtenay*, Oxford 1930

63. Gwynn, D., *O'Connell, Davis and the Colleges Bill*, Cork 1948

64. Gwynn, D., *Young Ireland and 1848*, Cork 1949

65. Hill, J., 'Nationalism and the Catholic Church in the 1840s: views of Dublin Repealers', *Irish Historical Studies* XIX, 1975

66. Hill, J., 'The Protestant Response to Repeal: the Case of the Dublin Working Class' in Lyons, F. S. L. and Hawkins, R. A. J., eds, *Ireland Under the Union: Varieties of Tension*, Oxford 1980

67. Holohan, P., 'Daniel O'Connell and the Dublin Trades: A Collision 1837—8', *Saothar* I, 1975

68. Inglis, B., 'O'Connell and the Irish Press 1800—42', *Irish Historical Studies* VIII, 1952

69. Jephson, H., *The Platform: Its Rise and Progress*, 2 vols, London 1892

70. Lyne, G. J., 'Daniel O'Connell, Intimidation and the Kerry Elections of 1835', *Kerry Archaeological and Historical Society* IV, 1974

71. McCaffrey, L. J., *Daniel O'Connell and the Repeal Year*, Kentucky 1966

72. McCartney, D., ed., *The World of Daniel O'Connell*, Dublin 1980

73. MacDonagh, O., 'The Contribution of O'Connell', in Farrell, B., ed., *The Irish Parliamentary Tradition*, Dublin 1973

[148]

74. MacDonagh, O., 'The Politicization of the Irish Catholic Bishops, 1800–50', *The Historical Journal* XVIII, 1975

75. McDowell, R. B., *Public Opinion and Government Policy in Ireland 1801–1846*, London 1953

76. Macintyre, A., *The Liberator: Daniel O'Connell and the Irish Party*, London 1965

77. Murphy, M., 'Municipal Reform and the Repeal Movement in Cork 1833–1844', *Journal of the Cork Historical and Archaeological Society* LXXXI, 1976

78. Murphy, M., 'Repeal, Popular Politics and the Catholic Clergy of Cork 1840–50', *Journal of the Cork Historical and Archaeological Society* LXXXII, 1977

79. Nowlan, K. B., 'The Catholic Clergy in Irish Politics in the Eighteen Thirties and Forties', *Irish Historical Studies* IX, 1974

80. Nowlan, K. B., 'The Meaning of Repeal in Irish History', *Historical Studies* IV, 1963

81. Nowlan, K. B., *The Politics of Repeal*, London 1965

82. O'Brien, J., *The Catholic Middle Classes in Pre-Famine Cork*, O'Donnell Lecture, National University of Ireland 1979

83. Ó Broin, L., 'The Trial and Imprisonment of O'Connell, 1843', *Éire-Ireland* VIII, 1973

84. *O'Connell Centenary Record, 1875*, Dublin 1878

85. O'Connell, M. R., 'Daniel O'Connell: income, expenditure and despair', *Irish Historical Studies* XVII, No. 66, 1970

86. O'Connell, M. R., 'Daniel O'Connell and the Irish Eighteenth Century', *Studies in Eighteenth-Century Culture* V, Wisconsin 1976

87. O'Connell, M. R., 'O'Connell Reconsidered', *Studies* LXIV, 1975

88. O'Connell, M. R., 'Daniel O'Connell and Religious Freedom', *Thought*, Vol. 50, 1975

89. O'Connell, M. R., 'O'Connell, Young Ireland, and Violence', *Thought*, Vol. 52, 1977

90. O'Ferrall, F., 'The Growth of Political Consciousness in Ireland 1823–1847', *Irish Economic and Social History* VI, 1979

91. O'Ferrall, F., 'The Struggle for Catholic Emancipation in County Longford 1824–29', *Teathbha* (Journal of the Longford Historical Society) I, No. 4, 1978

92. O'Flanagan, J. R., *The Bar Life of O'Connell*, Dublin 1875

93. O'Flanagan, J. R., *The Irish Bar*, London 1879
94. O'Flanagan, J. R., *The Munster Circuit*, London 1880 [149]
95. Osofsky, G., 'Abolitionists, Irish Immigrants, and the Dilemmas of Romantic Nationalism', *The American Historical Review* LXXX, 1975
96. Ó Tuathaigh, G., 'Gaelic Ireland, Popular Politics and Daniel O'Connell', *Journal of the Galway Archaeological and Historical Society*, XXXV, 1975
97. Ó Tuathaigh, G., *Thomas Drummond and the Government of Ireland 1835–41*, O'Donnell Lecture, National University of Ireland 1977
98. Reynolds, J. A., *The Catholic Emancipation Crisis in Ireland 1823–29*, New Haven 1954
99. Riach, D. C., 'Daniel O'Connell and American Anti-Slavery', *Irish Historical Studies*, XX, 1976
100. Shaw Lefevre, G. J., *Peel and O'Connell*, London 1887
101. Walsh, William J., *O'Connell, Archbishop Murray and the Board of Charitable Bequests*, Dublin 1916
102. Zimmermann, G. D., *Songs of Irish Rebellion: Political Street Ballads and Rebel Songs 1780–1900*, Dublin 1967

Index